DISCIPLESHIP DEFINED

DISCIPLESHIP DEFINED

Eric Russ

To the biggest display of God's grace in my life
next to Jesus Christ:

My wife, Sara,
and our children,
Connor, Joel, Lauren and Eli

TABLE OF CONTENTS

FOREWORD

Having finished his mission to redeem the world, Jesus sent his followers out to "make disciples of all nations" (Matt. 28:19). He amplified God's original commission to our forbearers in the garden of Eden to "be faithful and increase in numbers, fill the earth and subdue it" (Gen. 1:28).

In both commissions, God's purpose to raise up a faithful posterity across the earth is clear, as well as the way that objective would be accomplished by making reproducing disciples. The family is the model, both in giving birth to new believers and then training them in the mission of God.

Although Adam and Eve by their disobedience failed in their responsibility, the principles in raising children who would follow the Lord remained applicable through the Old Testament just as they are today (e.g. Deut. 6:4-9).

Jesus brings these relational principles supremely into focus as he pours his life into the development of his disciples. Then before returning to take his place of authority at the throne of God, he told his followers to replicate in their lives what he had been doing with them. That's what the Great Commission is all about.

Every redeemed sinner can have this ministry. It is the priesthood of all believers, making disciples is not some gift of the Spirit or a special call to the clergy; it is a lifestyle; it is the way Jesus lived among us, and now the way he calls his church to follow.

These life-transforming principles of disciple making learned from Jesus are always relevant, though they must be contextualized in society. Methods are conditioned by the culture in which people live.

That is why this book is so pertinent. Eric Russ gets down to where the rubber meets the road and offers some practical guidelines to observe where we live and work everyday.

Giving the book a ring of authenticity, Eric does not write as a theoretician but as a practitioner. He and his team have been planting a church through discipleship making in a very needy neighborhood in Detroit, Michigan. Not an easy task. But they have persevered to see a growing body of believers take root and reach out in love to their community.

The story is still in the making and one, which, I believe, will instruct and challenge the people to greater faithfulness in fulfilling Christ's last command to his church. It is therefore a pleasure to commend Discipleship Defined.

ROBERT COLEMAN, Ph.D.,
Author of *The Master Plan of Evangelism* and
Gordon-Conwell Theological Seminary
Distinguished Senior Professor of Discipleship and Evangelism

PREFACE

AN UNLIKELY DISCIPLE

I disregarded the screaming protests of the man's young children as I stood over his bloody and unconscious body and repeatedly delivered kicks to his face. Before I could kill him, my friend Chris pulled me off and ushered me back to the car where our dates were waiting. The man I just beat up had nearly hit our car while we were on our way to the senior prom, and I took it upon myself to teach him a lesson. This wasn't an uncommon occurrence to me. This was how I lived my life.

I grew up in inner city Cleveland, and as early as I can remember, my parents dealt drugs. My dad was involved in organized crime and would spend most of our money to feed his drug habit. My mom was an alcoholic and the angriest person I knew. My dad cheated on her and eventually beat her, so at age twelve, we left him.

By the time I reached high school, I was shaped into a hard and angry kid who was always getting into trouble. I gained a reputation for drug dealing, fighting, stealing and womanizing. Yet, there was another side of me. When I was eight, I was placed in the academic honors program at school. Even though I was a thug on the streets, I excelled in the classroom.

After I was arrested on the night of my senior prom, I told myself that I'd go to college and straighten out my life; I realized the path I was heading down would only lead to destruction. The next year I walked onto the campus of Miami University in Ohio hoping to change my criminal lifestyle. Haunted by old habits, it only took a week before I got into a couple of fistfights.

Throughout my first semester, people who talked about Jesus kept popping up in my life. A guy in my dorm named Mark started a Bible study, and my roommate Chris kept inviting me to come. Eventually, I did.

I always believed that God existed, but as I continued to go to these events where Jesus was proclaimed, I was forced to grapple with the fact that I did not have a relationship with Him. It was difficult because I grew up in a culture where Christianity was just a part of being black and a custom to be carried out on Sundays. With this baggage, concepts like life transformation and allegiance to Jesus were not just new to me, but intimidating. Yet, intellectually I knew that Jesus was king.

While at a conference sponsored by Campus Crusade for Christ, Jesus allowed me to put aside myself as an idol and submit to his love and lordship. I accepted Jesus.

For the next year, I did "Christian things" like studying the Bible and attending church, but I was still trying to figure out what it meant to really walk with the Lord. That's when I met Roger Hershey.

Roger was the director of Campus Crusade for Christ at Miami, an unassuming white guy who seemed genuinely interested in my life and my journey. He kept initiating opportunities to hang out with me and was always extending invitations for Christian events. I never saw someone with so much intentionality, so I was initially freaked out.

I spent the next two years being discipled by Roger. He would come to my dorm room and teach me the fundamental truths of Christianity. After studying the Word, he'd ask me questions and required that I show him where in the Bible I got the answers.

Often Roger went door to door throughout the dorms and set up meetings to talk with my peers. He'd share the Gospel with my friends and let me sit in on the conversation. Afterward, Roger would walk me through the conversation; he was training me on how to communicate my faith.

We spent so much time together, and Roger was always reminding me that he was training me so that I could make disciples of my own.

After college, I passed on a job offer from Procter and Gamble to pursue full time work with Campus Crusade for Christ because there was nothing I wanted to do more than share the Gospel. After a couple years on campus at Michigan State University, three years of seminary in Boston, a year in Uganda, and a few years working for a ministry in Cincinnati, my family and I moved to the east side of inner city Detroit. We planted Mack Avenue Community Church, and discipleship is the heartbeat of our ministry. I didn't want to introduce this book with a theological outline of discipleship, but a practical one. I could only be the man I am today because of the work God did through my discipleship relationship with Roger. Roger understood Jesus' call for us to make disciples, and his faithfulness ultimately led me to plant a church that focuses on making disciples.

I want you to build conviction that the creator of the universe wants us to make disciples. He commands it. And if my story is any indication, He uses it.

PART I
God's Thinking

WE AREN'T MAKING DISCIPLES

This book isn't meant to spark a revolution, but a return; it's a return to an idea (command, actually) that has gone ignored by many modern churches and Christians.[1]

Many churches view Christian discipleship as an alternative activity or an optional program, others view it as a spiritual gift that is tailor-made for someone with a specific call.

Do you want to know how Christ views discipleship? He views it as a mandate, not a preference. His ministry modeled it, and His last words instructed it. Even His followers in the early church understood the gravity of discipleship. But in Christian circles today, discipleship is either often misunderstood or just plain missing.

When we read our Bibles, we hastily glance over the Great Commission because we've heard it so many times. We sweep its meaning under the rug and insist that Jesus was just giving the disciples a little encouragement before He left. We're too afraid, or inept, to unpack what Jesus actually commanded, so discipleship remains undefined. The danger is that we're shying away from fulfilling our destinies in Christ.

It is my aim and prayer that this book helps us recognize the clear and forthright biblical reasons for discipleship. I hope that from reading this and investigating the scriptures on our own, we build a conviction that discipleship isn't a mere proclivity developed by super-Christians, but a charge given to all of us by our risen king.

WHAT DISCIPLESHIP ISN'T

If you're reading this book, you probably love the Lord. You go to church every Sunday. You have a good prayer life. You may attend a weekly Bible study. Heck, you may even have gone on a few mission trips.

But are you making disciples?

Discipleship is a popular word, often used vaguely and ambiguously but rarely used biblically. Many churches, even well-intentioned, God-fearing, Christ-loving, Bible-centered churches, muddle the definition of discipleship, and therefore abandon any intentionality of it. We know discipleship is something we should do, but either because we're not entirely sure what it is or because it'd be a "hard sell" to our congregations, we take a buckshot approach. We load up on Christian activities – training seminars, Bible studies, small groups, fellowship, conferences, etc. – in hope that discipleship will somehow magically take place along the way. We figure that if we blanket ourselves with church stuff, then somewhere in there we will have fulfilled Jesus' mandate to make disciples. Do we honestly believe that discipleship is supposed to be that truncated, that manufactured?

I'm not against Christian activities, nor am I attempting to indict your local church. I'm just concerned about how off-target our view of discipleship often is.

To give an example, someone once told me that we are always discipling each other, that discipleship is that which takes place when Christians are together. It could be an activity such as hanging out at a Starbucks or exercising together. For him, anything geared toward seeing a person move one step closer to Jesus is considered discipleship.

I don't necessarily disagree with this claim, but the broad strokes with which my friend painted discipleship is dangerous, and it affirmed my suspicion that discipleship has become undefined in many of our churches and Christian organizations.

Let me illustrate further. When I ask various church leaders if their people are being discipled, I often hear the answer, "Yes, we have small group Bible studies," or, "Of course," and then the leaders proceed to back up their answers by listing off programs like Sunday school and prayer meetings. The implication here is that small group Bible study is equivalent to discipleship. These programs could be components of discipleship, but do they act as a convincing demonstration of what Christ meant when he told us to make disciples? These questions can't be answered without having a standard by which to go.

If there is no clear standard of what discipleship is, then it becomes difficult to determine if we're doing discipleship or not. While we have obfuscated the definition of discipleship, Jesus was never equivocal about His vision. When He commanded us to go and make disciples of all nations, He had a clear picture of what it should look like.

So far, we've discussed how the church has frequently missed the mark when it comes to discipleship. Now we need to discus that mark by understanding what first-century Jews, particularly Jesus, thought about discipleship.

THE BIBLICAL RATIONALE FOR DISCIPLESHIP

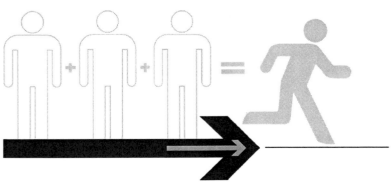

THE *OLD* UNDERSTANDING OF DISCIPLE

"Disciple" is derived from the Greek word μαθητεύω that means, "to learn," and it also can be used as a name for a pupil or follower of a teacher. Pupils, by definition, adopt the distinctive teaching of their masters, the term signifying one who adheres to a particular religious or philosophical worldview. This is why "Disciple" can be used to describe those who responded to Jesus' message (Mt. 5:1; Lk. 6:17; 19:37), but it can also refer more specifically to those who accompanied him on his travels (Mk. 6:45; Lk. 8:2f.; 10:1), and especially to the twelve apostles (Mk. 3:14).

Historically, the term "disciple" speaks to the recognition of a pupil-teacher relationship. In regard to its usage in scripture, it is important to understand that Jesus essentially redefined the term "disciple." A disciple of Jesus wasn't only a follower of His teachings; it involved personal allegiance to Him, expressed by following Him and pledging exclusive loyalty (Mk. 8:34-38; Lk. 14:26-33). In every case, readiness to pronounce the claims of Jesus at any cost was demanded. Jesus offered Himself, rather than His outstanding gifts, and desired allegiance to Him, rather than to a cause that He represented.[1] Such an attitude went well beyond the normal pupil-teacher relationship and gave the word "disciple" a new sense.[2]

You might be thinking, "Okay, so that's what Jesus thinks it means to be a disciple, but how do we *make* disciples?"

Don't worry. Jesus told us how we should do it. Let's look at how He made disciples.

ONE GREAT COMMISSION?

Historically, the plan for discipleship has been clearly expressed through the Great Commission (Mt. 28:18-20). However, we should recognize that the Great Commission is not an isolated mandate. Although Matthew 28 can stand firmly on its own, Jesus explicitly reveals His plan for discipleship throughout the gospels, specifically in the commissions found at the end of each gospel and at the beginning of Acts.[3]

Matthew 28:18-20
[18]Then Jesus came to them and said, "All authority in heaven and on earth has been given to me. [19]Therefore go and make disciples of all nations, baptizing them in the name of the Father and of the Son and of the Holy Spirit, [20]and teaching them to obey everything I have commanded you. And surely I am with you always, to the very end of the age."

Mark 16:15-16
[15]He said to them, "Go into all the world and preach the gospel to all creation. [16]Whoever believes and is baptized will be saved, but whoever does not believe will be condemned.

Luke 24:46-49
[46]He told them, "This is what is written: The Messiah will suffer and rise from the dead on the third day, [47]and repentance for the forgiveness of sins will be preached in his name to all nations, beginning at Jerusalem. [48]You are witnesses of these things. [49]I am going to send you what my Father has promised; but stay in the city until you have been clothed with power from on high."

John 20:21
Again Jesus said, "Peace be with you! As the Father has sent me, I am sending you."

Acts 1:7-8
[7]He said to them: "It is not for you to know the times or dates the Father has set by his own authority. [8]But you will receive power when the Holy Spirit comes on you; and you will be my witnesses

in Jerusalem, and in all Judea and Samaria, and to the ends of the earth."

As we take a closer look at these exhortations, the importance should be clear. First, we should note that these five phrases are said near the conclusion of Jesus' stay with his disciples. When someone says their last words, people tend to listen extra carefully. Last words are generally thought of as important and meant to be remembered. Considering the situation, we must say the same holds true for Jesus. He chose his words carefully, and because they are of his last, we should take special notice.

It is undisputed that Jesus' urgings are given in a variety of settings after the resurrection. This reveals that Jesus did not just proclaim one commission to be later described differently by different authors, but that He made this same kind of declaration at least four different times at four different locations, emphasizing the seriousness of the charge (not counting the ambiguous setting of Mark 16)[4]. It's reasonable to conclude that "making disciples" was probably the most important request that Jesus had for His followers.

The reason that we have appointed Matthew 28:18-20 to be the great commission isn't because it's the only commission given by Jesus before His departure, but it's the one that embodies the aspects of all the others (specifically, being empowered by God, being sent, preaching, being on mission, and teaching).

JESUS' COMMAND

In Matthew 28:18-20, we read "Then Jesus came to them and said, 'All authority in heaven and on earth has been given to me. Therefore go and make disciples of all nations, baptizing them in the name of the Father and of the Son and of the Holy Spirit, and teaching them to obey everything I have commanded you. And surely I am with you always, to the very end of the age.'"

After Jesus' resurrection, all authority was entrusted to Him. He does not wait passively in heaven for his glorious arrival as king, but already He exercises his lordship.

In order to build a firm foundation for our discussion, let's use a little academic jargon and spend a brief moment unpacking the notion of us now being commanded to disciple.

At first glance, it may appear that this passage has many commands. Grammatically, however, there is only one command in this whole passage, and that command is surrounded by three participles. The one command being communicated is simply, Make Disciples. The first participle "πορευθέντες" or "going/traveling" is one of attendant circumstance.[5] That means it is used to communicate an action that is coordinate with the finite verb, in this case "μαθητεύσατε" or, "you disciple." Because of this, the verb is not a dependent verb and is best translated "go and make." Therefore, in Matthew's mind, while being commanded to make disciples, "go" is understood as not only a nonnegotiable but as an assumptive action, always working in tandem with the command "μαθητεύσατε." Plainly, Jesus is saying to all who recognize His lordship: wherever you go and whenever you go, be *making disciples*.

"βαπτίζοντες" or "baptizing" and "διδάσκοντες" or "teaching" are participles of means. Jesus is communicating how the action of the finite verb "μαθητεύσατε" is accomplished.[6] First, let's look at "baptizing." By using "βαπτίζοντες," Jesus is describing the initiation into his fold. The focus is witnessing, so the task of baptizing in this text is mainly an evangelistic task. Also assumed in "baptizing" was the thought of immersing professing Christians in water as a public display of their allegiance to Christ.[7] However, it was understood that the physical immersion represented a theological assumption of initiation into the family of God. Said differently, baptism finds its fulfillment in ministry, which God uses to bring people out of the family of Satan and into His.

The second participle of means is "teaching." Jesus wants us to teach disciples all that He has commanded. The heart of "διδάσκοντες" is to "train and catechize," so the main thrust is educational. By teaching what Jesus taught, the church becomes an extension of His ministry. In all, the command to disciple finds its fulfillment in evangelism and education. Education must not be simply digesting theology, but equipping people to obey all that Jesus commanded.

The command "to obey all..." may sound overwhelming (if viewed from the Pharisee's point of view). Thankfully, Jesus is not requiring the disciples to complete a checklist in order to please God. Rather, Jesus is requiring that they be fully devoted to Him and completely depend on His leadership and power to accomplish His plan. This is why He says, "And surely I am with you always, to the very end of the age."

Put simply, Jesus is asking his disciples to carry the mantle in the following way:

- He is assuming that we are *going.*
- And while we go, we need to *make disciples.*
- The way we make disciples is by:
  - o *Baptizing* – giving people the opportunity who do not identify with the family of God to be initiated into His family.
  - o *Teaching* – learning and modeling in our lives all that Jesus proclaimed, commanded and modeled.
  - o The only reason we are able to do this is because *Jesus sent us* to do it, and *Jesus will be with us* while we do it.

Be encouraged. Jesus didn't just give us this commission without a practical demonstration. We can mimic his ministry.

JESUS' PRACTICAL MODEL OF THIS COMMAND

Discipleship was Jesus' method of winning the world to Himself. In fact, despite His popularity (5,000 men gathering to hear Him speak is no joke!), it is clear that Jesus did not focus on the temporal admiration of men, but quietly poured His life in those who would multiply. As Dr. Robert Coleman once said, Jesus staked His whole ministry on twelve men. He was not trying to impress the crowd, but usher in the kingdom.[8]

The gospels as a whole reveal that Christ expects His followers to be fruitful (Jn. 15:16). He knew that he would have to equip the saints to be able to lead the multitudes. The evidence is conclusive in the gospels that discipleship as described above was foundational to Jesus' ministry.

Jesus' subsequent followers saw how Jesus discipled others, heeded His command, and joyfully took up the call to do the same.

THE EARLY CHURCH MODEL OF THE COMMAND

The apostles of the early church took Jesus' command seriously. One clear example is the life that Paul modeled, shown most beautifully by the exhortation given in 2 Timothy 2:2.

Paul met Timothy on his second visit to Lystra and the two quickly became friends. Paul took Timothy under his wing as a disciple and even referred to him as his son in the faith. Paul trained his disciple in ministry and even ordained him. Later, when Paul was in prison, he wrote to Timothy, "And the things you have heard me say in the presence of many witnesses, entrust to reliable men who will also be qualified to teach others."

Paul understood the necessity of discipleship. He poured his life into Timothy and encouraged him to continue the process. While being sent, Timothy was to continue the legacy by sending other faithful men out who would eventually send others, and so on.

Again, the evidence consistently shows that discipleship was a mandate from Christ, one to be followed by all those who sail under His flag.

WHY WE DISCIPLE

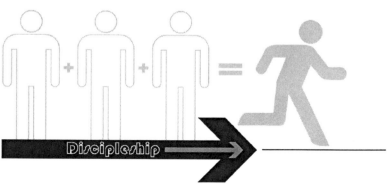

Jesus didn't just give this command to his early disciples; He was talking to you and me. He expected the Christians of today to carry out the commission. Why? Because we're the sent ones.

THE SENT ONES

There is a phrase that I commonly use when referring to Christians: the "sent people of God." It is one of the most important themes of scripture. Jesus said in John 20:21, "Peace be with you! As the Father has sent me, I am sending you." The point that Jesus is making to His disciples—and us—is that we are not only being sent by Him, but we are continuing as His representatives on earth, allowing us to participate in the narrative of redemptive history that He authors. The scriptural support for this point is overwhelming.

John 13:20
I tell you the truth, whoever accepts anyone I send accepts me; and whoever accepts me accepts the one who sent me.

Matthew 15:24
He answered, "I was sent only to the lost sheep of Israel."

Mark 3:14
He appointed twelve—designating them apostles—that they might be with him and that he might send them out to preach.

Luke 10:2

He told them, "The harvest is plentiful, but the workers are few. Ask the Lord of the harvest, therefore, to send out workers into his harvest field.

God sent the Israelites out into the world to be a light and to proclaim their God as the true God, with the desired result of having the other nations longing to worship Israel's God (Gal. 3:8). Unfortunately, Israel was not the light that they were supposed to be (Ezek. 36:22-23).

Because of this, the Father sent Jesus to accomplish what Israel could not—to be chosen, be sent, and to proclaim. Just as the Father sent Jesus, Jesus then sent his apostles to proclaim His coming and resurrection (Is. 42:6). The apostles then sent disciples out into the world, and so on. In fact, John 20:21 shows that the work of proclaiming the Gospel is ultimately Christ's own work; He just gives the disciples a share of it through sending them. As it was with the Father to the Son, the success of the apostles is the success of Jesus Himself (Lk. 10:17).

As Jesus' supporting cast, we are called to retell the triumphant story of the cross with the way we live our lives (through word and deed). The frequency of the subject's appearance in scripture suggests that God does not want us to forget this important theme. It is our honor to be a part of Christ's legacy, to bear the title, "The Sent Ones."

We cannot trick ourselves into thinking that the Great Commission doesn't apply to us, that Jesus' words weren't meant for our ears. Let us build the conviction that when Jesus said to "make disciples," He was saying it with *us* in mind.

THE REAL ISSUE

Jesus' command to disciple is revealed throughout the scriptures, and He expects everyone under his allegiance to carry it out. Although that is clear, there is some room for discrepancy in what this command entails. The question then becomes, how are we supposed to disciple?

Let me give an example. A pastor, who is also a dear friend of mine, wanted me to assist him in implementing discipleship in his church. After getting to know the church body, I pointed out to him that people were not being trained on how to talk to others about Jesus and that there was not a culture of faithfully studying the scriptures, despite the existence of Bible studies in their church. I also told him that although many people within the body had relationships, the relationships were founded on sharing similar hobbies and enjoying each other's company, rather than connecting with the goal of yielding to Christ. There was no ethos to make sure that the relationships had the juice to be redemptive.

His response was to defend the church body, first by pointing out the handful of members that were super-motivated in walking with the Lord, and then casting these tendencies across the entire body. Then he contended that all of their church activities were discipleship. His defense not only misrepresented the DNA of the church but also the meaning of discipleship.

Needless to say, we never revisited the discussion. My pastor friend didn't implement discipleship and didn't even dialogue with me about what that meant for his church.

If he really thought that everything is discipleship, where is the metric to indicate if we are discipling well or not? How do we know if Jesus is pleased?

It seems irresponsible to go through our Christian walks convinced that Jesus' metrics of discipleship are too blurry. By unpacking the commission, it should be clear to us that God has indeed given us a standard, clearly articulated by Jesus. Even so, do we know how to go around baptizing and teaching? Although it takes some work, we must aim to contextualize the commission of Matthew 28 in its first-century vernacular so it can meet us in today's covenant community. We can achieve this by grasping Jesus' expectations for discipleship in three categories:[1]

- **Word** (Jn. 15:7, 5:38; Lk. 11:28, 8:11; Mk 4:14)
  o Teaching disciples to obey all that Christ commanded and modeled throughout the scriptures

- **Ministry** (Lk. 10; Mt 24:14; Mk 16; Jn. 7:4-24)
  o Training disciples in service and evangelism

- **Relationship** (Jn. 1:43; 11:54; 1:17; Mt 9:9; Lk. 22:41)
  o Building relationships that feature love, commitment, and intentionality

If an individual or a ministry claims to be discipling people, yet lacks one of these three components, it would be fair to conclude that they are not providing the holistic discipleship that Jesus modeled, commissioned, and expected. Let's take a look at how Jesus' expectations flow from these metrics.

THE WORD IN DISCIPLESHIP

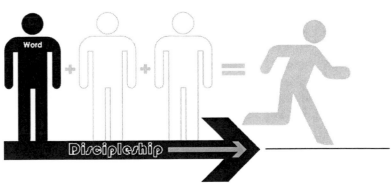

C ontrary to many sects and movements that misrepresent the origin of truth, we obtain our instruction not through emotion, but through Jesus, by way of the scriptures.

Jesus asked us to make disciples and *teach them* everything He commanded. This implies that we have to train disciples in how to read the Bible. Let's look at a few verses that speak to the importance of Jesus' words.

Nehemiah 8:7-8

[7]The Levites—Jeshua, Bani, Sherebiah, Jamin, Akkub, Shabbethai, Hodiah, Maaseiah, Kelita, Azariah, Jozabad, Hanan and Pelaiah—instructed the people in the Law while the people were standing there. [8]They read from the Book of the Law of God, making it clear and giving the meaning so that the people could understand what was being read.

John 5:38

Nor does his word dwell in you, for you do not believe the one he sent.

Luke 11:28

He replied, "Blessed rather are those who hear the word of God and obey it."

1 Tim. 4:13

Until I come, devote yourself to the public reading of Scripture, to preaching and to teaching.

Hebrews 4:12

For the word of God is living and active. Sharper than any double-edged sword, it penetrates even to dividing soul and spirit, joints and marrow; it judges the thoughts and attitudes of the heart.

2 Tim 2:15

Do your best to present yourself to God as one approved, a workman who does not need to be ashamed and who correctly handles the word of truth.

THE TRUTH DILEMMA

We are a biblically illiterate culture and it is getting worse. Don't mistake this statement as hyperbole. George Barna has conducted research on the matter, and the results are alarming. Fewer than half of all adults can name the four gospels. Many Christians cannot identify more than two or three of the disciples. Twelve percent of adults believe that Joan of Arc was Noah's wife. Sixty percent of Americans can't name even five of the Ten Commandments. Barna comments, "No wonder people break the Ten Commandments all the time. They don't know what they are."[1] It's an understatement to say that our culture is biblically illiterate. Unless we do something, the trend will only continue to spiral downward.

This illiteracy has lulled our minds and made us complacent, even apathetic, when we approach the scriptures. The notion of standing firm in the truth of scripture has been deemed by some Christians as narrow-minded and void of heart. Neither is true.

As Christians, we must concede that we can't have a discussion about growing in the Lord without discussing the need to know His Word. We are commanded to know His Word, store it in our hearts, and guard it carefully. A variety of methods are welcomed, but in every method the principles must remain the same: Learning how to read and study the Bible and allowing the revealed truths to be appropriately applied to one's life.

The principle of learning and applying God's Word is nonnegotiable. Jesus showed His disciples the importance of the Holy Scriptures, referring to them in both His own personal devotion and in His ministry to win others to Himself. In the four gospels, when Jesus was in dialogue with His disciples, He made numerous references to the Old Testament. When speaking to others, Jesus made almost one hundred Old Testament allusions. In the same way, churches and individuals should view scripture as an integral component in growing as a disciple of Christ. Anyone who wishes to make disciples should have a love for the scriptures and a desire to impart that love on the people they are discipling.

Even though we have such a clear model in Christ, we are approaching a dangerous time in history. I fear that our passion for ministering to a culture that hides from truth has caused us to question truth's importance. I have been in Bible studies where the leader has said, "Now tell us what this passage means to you" or "What insight did you gain from this passage?" If it's our desire to cultivate faithful Bible study habits, these are the wrong questions to ask. In fact, these questions enhance the sneaky postmodern thinking that has invaded our worldview—the idea that there are many different truths, and that the standard is founded on what an individual gets out of it. Whether this approach is intentional or not, it spawns a society of Bible readers that is unconcerned about the authors' intended meaning of the text. If we continue down this path, the Bible will transform from a Spirit-inspired historical document that tells the story of God into a self-help manual that helps us better our lives.

This lack of concern is proof that the importance of doctrine is a subject that needs to be addressed with a sense of urgency.

I remember having a discussion with a buddy of mine that frustratingly admitted that he did not like studying the Bible, because he feared that it would make him too intellectual and would curtail his passion for Christ. He felt that the intellectual component got in the way of pure devotion. His assertion concerns me, but what concerns me even more is the fact that more and more Christians are expressing similar sentiments.

I've heard Christians jokingly refer to seminaries as cemeteries. The punchline infers that by spending a lot of time studying and training, one's zeal for Christ dies, and that those institutions dedicated to equipping people for service to God somehow squeeze out their passion for Him.

While there exists a realistic danger of being puffed-up by knowledge, this hazard has led too many people to the inaccurate conclusion that doctrine shouldn't be considered that important in one's relationship with God. Over the last few generations, doctrine and devotion have been unfairly pitted against each other as enemies. However, Jesus never viewed these two elements as having an antagonistic relationship. He saw them as complements, both working together in harmony toward the goal of glorifying God.

In order to realign ourselves, we must first survey the importance of correct doctrine. Doctrine is one of the cornerstones of discipleship. Without a deep conviction of its importance, discipleship is rendered unfaithful and incomplete. Hopefully, this discussion will encourage us to hold true to that which God has entrusted to us.

Exposing The Bible Literacy Disconnect

There are many church leaders that truly love God and the people they serve. They readily affirm the importance of truth and are devoted to faithfully serving the Lord and His people, but too often do they develop biblically illiterate followers of Christ.

The illiteracy usually begins from the subtle ways that the ethos of our Christian walks is established. We need to watch where we encourage fellow Christians to obtain information on spiritual matters. We like to point people to popular Christian books, but how often do we point them to the Bible? Know that I am not advocating a "Bible only" mentality. However, by recommending the former rather than the latter, we are promoting the idea that extra-biblical resources surpass the importance of the Bible itself. We have to first make sure that the scriptures are seen in proper perspective if we are to develop biblically literate Christians.

One of the most prevalent ways that churches and leaders raise biblically illiterate Christians is by redefining devotion. The new devotion philosophy maintains that life is about loving Jesus in an emotional and super-spiritual way, and that pursuing wisdom through avenues of personal study and theological discussion impedes the deep, spiritual connection.

My wife recently spent time with her friend who attends a church we used to serve. This church has several strengths, but one glaring weakness is how it views Bible study. No one in the church would ever claim to have a low view of scripture, yet the church would regularly have Bible studies without even opening the Bible! My wife's friend remarked, "I value my relational time so much that I consider it way more important than filling my head with knowledge."

While it's great to hear that this woman values relationships, she's biblically off-base in her assertion that knowledge of scripture necessarily conflicts with them. This sentiment, which places an extreme focus on relationships, cultivates the mentality that studying scripture isn't a priority in the development of a believer.

This is a sad reality that I have experienced many times. In the past, even some church leaders have responded negatively when they heard about my emphasis on theology and passion for pursuing knowledge of God. Seeking and receiving sound doctrine is key for us to progress as followers of Jesus. If we've had past experiences where scripture was minimized or misleading, we mustn't let it deter us from consistently approaching the Word.

Satan's Lies Keep Us From Truth

As we pursue truth in scripture, we must consider that Satan's job is to deceive. Satan tests God's people by manipulating circumstances within the limits that God allows him in an attempt to make them desert God's will (Gen 3:4; Jb. 1:12; 2:6; 1 Cor. 10:13). The Bible teaches that we must be consistently watchful for, aware of, and active against the devil and his schemes to make us fall. (Mk. 14:38; 2 Cor. 2:11; Eph. 6:10ff.; Jas. 4:7; 1 Pet. 5:9). Deception is Satan's favorite tool. He tries to misrepresent who God is by blurring God's truth and will for us (Gn. 3:1-5; 2 Cor. 11:3,14; Mt. 4:5ff.).

Because of Satan's deceitfulness, this is where Bible study finds itself today. Within the body of believers, there is a distorted view of God, His word, and His will. We must reveal the schemes of Satan and live in light of Truth. The Truth of God, found in scripture, is the light that allows us to see, the guide that enables us to understand our lives and this world. We must flex our capacity to say "no" to the lies of Satan and to celebrate the truth of God's Word.

GETTING BACK ON TRACK: MAXIMIZING BIBLE STUDY

The traditional Bible study generally consists of a group gathering to discuss a book, theme, or passage in the Bible. The group has a designated leader who facilitates discussion and tries to foster an environment where people feel connected.

The desire for communal love and time in the Bible are aspects of the generic model that are healthy for the growth of a believer. However, what seems to be missing here is the intentionality of training and guarding truth. It is important that we restructure our Bible studies to ensure that people are not just reading the Bible but that they are learning *how* to read it, and learning how to teach others to do the same. This means that we must teach Bible study skills as we teach the Bible. In order for leaders to be able to healthily equip disciples, they need to know how to handle and teach truth.

In addition to what typical Bible study offers, our goal is to train people so that they may eventually become self-feeders and ultimately be able to teach others. Through faithful and intentional training of how to understand scripture, it is ensured that we, and generations to follow, will have the capacity to be heralds and stewards of God's truth.

The Scriptures teach the extreme importance of guarding our doctrine closely and the importance of learning and digesting God's truth in order to produce healthy disciples. At the same time, the Word must not be the only focus in discipleship, because then it would simply be a Bible study. Although a consistent, healthy diet of God's truth is a component of discipleship, it by no means comprises all of what discipleship is meant to be. Discipleship must also encompass ministry and community before we can be confident in labeling it a holistic model.

MINISTRY IN DISCIPLESHIP

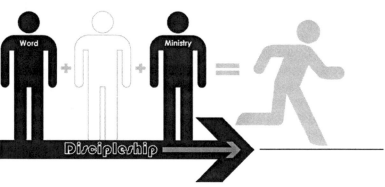

THE PROBLEM OF OUTSOURCING MINISTRY

Outsourcing has become a household term. It describes huge corporations contracting work abroad so they can be as effective and efficient as possible by making more products for a cheaper price. Like these corporations, the Christian community has been outsourcing ministry.

Imagine if only a small fraction of Christians preached the Gospel, but the results were exponential. Do you think Jesus would be cool with that? Well, He's not.

The redemptive story told throughout the Bible reveals that Jesus is just as passionate about the process of ministry as He is about its results. Let's start with a subtle example on how out-sourcing ministry can hinder what God wants to do in the world.

The Alpha Course has been designed to be a tool to bring people into discussion about the true meaning of life. In about ten weeks, the program enables many discussions that lead people to Christ. Over two million people have taken the course in the US.[1] The Lord is using this program tremendously.

My concern is not with Alpha specifically (it's proven to be a great tool for God's kingdom), but the mindset that effectiveness is more important than faithfulness. Similar programs end up not simply being great tools, but sadly, they become opportunities to outsource a necessary aspect of what it means to be a Christian, namely, to proclaim Christ.

I once served at a church where we implemented the Alpha program. As time went on, it became our sole evangelistic tool. It got to the point where ministry was equivalent to inviting people to run through the program. This church had no training for people to learn how to share their faith. We did not provide any intentional opportunities for people to model the Gospel in ministry and service. In essence, evangelism was outsourced to a program that left people not having to worry about witnessing themselves. No one was encouraged to go out and tell others about Jesus.

Even with church members sitting on the sidelines, multitudes heard the Gospel and many became followers of Christ. So what's the problem? While the people of this church loved the Lord and greatly desired people to know Him, the program became the primary means of outreach. When this occurs we run the risk of communicating the message that God is concerned only about the end product (people becoming Christians) and not how ministry itself bears God's image in the process. On the contrary, the scriptures clearly demonstrate that Jesus is concerned about both the process and end result of ministry.

First, and most important, is the biblical theme of bearing God's image through retelling Jesus' story. The Lord makes us His children, but at the same time, He makes us His missionaries. This is a legacy that includes God sending Jesus, Jesus sending the disciples and the disciples sending other people. To not train God's people and put them in situations to fulfill the mandate to proclaim Jesus to the world is in direct disobedience to his command to make Jesus known.

I also want to appeal to what Christ desires to do in our character through ministry. It seems only good things come out of people taking steps to make Christ known. To regularly proclaim God in the world grows people in their faith, gives them courage, and continually builds eternal perspective. When ministry happens, your theology finally has feet.

To be a man or woman who proclaims Jesus consistently in this world is like a faith steroid. God uses it to build the muscles of believers for the fight of faith and to make us more like Jesus. God has called us to retell His story and that is to be a missionary to the world, reminding it that there is a king and his name is Jesus. When we outsource this opportunity, we disregard obedience and shortchange what God wants to do in our lives.

If ministry is this important for the believer, then what is hindering us as a people of God?

MINISTRY: CHRISTIANTY 2.0?

For many Christians, ministry is the hardest aspect of Jesus' command to be faithful to, even though it's one of the main ways we fulfill his reason for recreating us. This is not popular among those of us who think we get saved to simply fall in love with Jesus, or those of us that facilitate an unnecessary tension between devotion and ministry. Too many of us view ministry as optional and radical – some sort of Christianity 2.0.

There is a movement of personal piety going around today that is hindering the Gospel, saying that it's meant solely for the person who receives it. But God didn't die for one person, nor did He die for just humans. His death and resurrection was to make right all creation. Personal devotion is extremely important, but we have to figure out a way to talk appropriately about devotion without placing ministry far in the background. The days must be over of seeing the Gospel being personal salvation and comfort, while the life of a missionary is to be a future elective that we can enroll in for extra-credit or simply choose to opt out of. That is not the story Jesus told with his life, words, or commands.

Ministering to the world allows us to be who we were created to be. Our personal piety works in tandem with our desire to display it to the world so that Christ might be famous. The goal of sanctification is not to just be pious. Ministry is not optional; it's not Christianity 2.0. It's the essence of the redeemed life. We must build our conviction toward this end. It seems most prudent to attempt this feat by trying to understand ministry from its roots – the Gospel.

FIRST THINGS FIRST: BIBLICAL BELIEF

The first step in understanding ministry is to comprehend Biblical belief. What does the Gospel/biblical belief have to do with ministry? Everything! Our understanding of recreation is paramount to our understanding of what we are to do with our lives as newly created humans (Christians).

It seems that today when people "get saved" from their sins, the focus is increasingly more man-centered. This is one of the many reasons we tend to overemphasize the notion that "God will save me if I simply believe." This philosophy leaves many thinking that salvation is simply "believing," while the definition of "believing" has become progressively more subjective.

Statements such as "Repent for the kingdom is here" and "Jesus will save you from your sins" are thrown around flippantly. However, when Jesus and his followers said these words, it was loaded with meaning. These phrases infer that Jesus has the authority and the power to save. There are two ways to respond to such radical claims. Reject it, or repent and believe. Rejection is usually seen as the intense denial of God's claims. But a more accurate picture of rejection, according to Christ, is anything other than repentance. This rejection can be dogmatic or involuntary, but anyone who does not enter into repentance has rejected the veracity of Christ's claim that "unless you repent, you too will all perish" (Luke 13:3).

Biblical repentance is not merely feeling sorry for sinning, but a complete alteration of the motivation and direction of one's life (Mt. 3:2, 11; Mk. 1:4; Lk. 3:3, 8; Acts 13:24,19:4). This new focus means to acknowledge that no one has claim upon God and submitting to His mercy (Lk. 18:13). No matter how many different ways the Gospel is presented, it demands the same response: a total reorientation to life according to the person of Jesus.

Getting saved from your sins was exactly what Jesus meant, but he also meant so much more — a total surrender to His rule and His ways. Jesus taught that under His rule our life indeed is no longer our own (1Cor. 6:19-20). This mindset is what God assumes and requires to all those who profess to follow Jesus (Mt. 10:37-39). This understanding and affirmation of the Gospel is the backdrop of Christian obedience.

It is important that we understand obedience not as the world does but as Jesus does. It's not that you have to live a life focused on duty and performance, but the opposite. There is nothing we can do to earn God's love or achieve salvation. Nobody can boast about earning God's favor, as it is an undeserved gift. Our works should only be motivated by the love and salvation God has already given us through Jesus. Jesus advocates good works, assuming they are done with the right motivation. When our actions are motivated by the love of God, then our works flow through the gift given to us by God—not as an attempt to earn it. The strength to do works comes from God, and the praise for these works goes to God. When we understand how much Christ loves us, we are enabled to fully partake in the ministry that God has for us. Consider the following verses:

Matthew 5:16
In the same way, let your light shine before men, that they may see your good deeds and praise your Father in heaven.

Ephesians 2:10
For we are God's workmanship, created in Christ Jesus to do good works, which God prepared in advance for us to do.

Romans 14:5-8
[5]One man considers one day more sacred than another; another man considers every day alike. Each one should be fully convinced in his own mind. [6]He who regards one day as special, does so to the Lord. He who eats meat, eats to the Lord, for he gives thanks to God; and he who abstains, does so to the Lord and gives thanks to God. [7]For none of us lives to himself alone and none of us dies to himself alone. [8]If we live, we live to the Lord; and if we die, we die to the Lord. So, whether we live or die, we belong to the Lord.

God doesn't simply want us to do something; he has made us someone. He has made us His child and His missionary to the world. Another joy of the Gospel is that we are able to see what joy-filled, grace-focused obedience looks like by taking our cue from Jesus, our great missionary. Jesus came from the realm of Heaven to Earth and made himself available to engage culture with the desire to make the Father known. He came to tell the world that the king is here and we may reign with him. Those whom the Father allows to respond in turn are born again as God's children and then are sent in this world with the purpose of telling it about who God is and what He has done for his creation and how all people can experience relationship with their creator. By worshipping Jesus and making worshippers for Jesus we fulfill our destinies as God's creation.

Salvation is not simply for us; it's mainly for God. God unleashes His new creation in the world to create and build worshippers. John Piper says it best, "Missions exist because worship doesn't."[2] All to say, radically obeying Christ's commands to carry the mantle as a missionary is not an option but a natural conclusion to our affirmation as Christ followers.

THE PROCESS OF MINISTRY

Ministry = Service + Evangelism

Ministry is the process that God uses to reconcile people to Himself. The Bible calls those things that we do for the glory of God "good works." All "good works" can be placed in two categories: service and evangelism. Even though we will discuss these categories separately, they are by no means exclusive of one another. Done prayerfully, they work together to bring recognition to God. We separate the two to provide clarity and understanding to the subject of ministry.

Service

The problem with service isn't that we necessarily lack a desire to do it, but it's that we often inaccurately define it. When we think about service, our mind usually wanders to a soup kitchen or serving the poor in a third world country. These assumptions are understandable, though incomplete.

Service, simply, is any activity done with the motivation to honor Jesus. Everything we do, we do unto the Lord. This reality should free us, motivate us, and challenge us not to dismiss buying a coworker a cup of coffee because it doesn't feel missional. To be clear, being a godly business executive or a godly dad is not second tier ministry. God is pleased with those works, and they are paramount.

With that said, we must not misuse this truth to cushion ourselves with freedom to practice emotional, physical, materialistic and spiritual gluttony. Not while the hurting continue to hurt. We bear the responsibility not to forget about God's concern for those who have been marginalized by society and affected by injustice.

Too seldom do we see the church give much thought (and action) to the kingdom of God as the Bible calls for (Pr. 29:7, 28:27, 21:13). In fact, from Old Testament Law (Ex. 22:21-21; Lev. 23:22, 25:39-43; Deut. 15:7-11) to Proverbs (Pro. 14:21, 31, 21:13) to the Gospels (Mt. 19:21) to the Epistles (Js. 1:26-27; Gal.2:10), God continually proclaims His care for the marginalized. He consistently seeks justice and makes provision for those who are hurting spiritually and physically, and He has commanded us to do the same (1 Tim 5:17-19).

Whether we know it or not, Platonic theory has crept into Christian thinking. Plato believed that physical realities were only superficial coverings of the internal soul, which represents reality. This is not the case in Christianity. While the believer is exhorted to live for eternal purposes, and not just temporary, the body, and creation in general, are never passed off as something to be ignored. It is never said, or even hinted at in the Bible, that the poor should just ignore their poverty and unjust systems should be left alone because the soul is the only thing that matters and physical needs don't.

Recently we have seen polarized positions between the Gospel message and the so-called "social Gospel." It has never been acceptable to make a distinction between the two as Christians. Perhaps we witness secular groups that promote helping others and we fear being identified with them, and therefore react by solely trying to help a person's spiritual needs. Just because some secularists have rejected the precious truth of Christ does not mean that we alter God's kingdom agenda in retaliation. We stay the course in pursuing God's holistic kingdom agenda in both spiritual matters and in social matters, fulfilling our role as agents of new creation (Pr. 31:8-9, 22:22-23, 19:17, 14:31). To simply teach doctrine and how to communicate faith without throwing down the challenge to love others and strive for justice would be a lethargic effort of modeling the ministry of Christ.

Intentionally serving others with the heart of God is the first nuance of ministry. However, if any person or church claims to have a ministry and is not helping those who are needy, they have missed a big portion of what it means to operate as image-bearers. Service to the poor, needy, and marginalized is part of the "good works" that God allows us to partake in. We must never lose sight of service as we move on to discuss the second component of ministry.

Evangelism

When we reflect on evangelism, there exists an interesting dilemma. The reality is that the cross is God's supreme self-revelation, but it occurred two thousand years ago. So how does God reveal Himself in the present with the supreme self-disclosure act of the past? The answer to this question brings us to the essence of evangelism—it is the timeless link between God's redemptive act and man's grasping of it. It is the medium through which God contemporizes His historic self-disclosure in Christ and offers man the opportunity to respond in faith.

Christ's command was plain. He wants all those who recognize Him as savior to preach the Gospel to all people. However, evangelism is much bigger than being a command in scripture; it is the story of God. God's desire to redeem is motivated by His love for His creation (Mt. 9:35-38; Eph 2:1-10).

Through evangelism, God allows us to join Him in His redemption and recreation through reconciling us to Himself and using us to reconcile others (2 Corinthians 5:18-21). His gracious act is ultimately creating a people for Himself who profess God amidst a world that hates Him. This end goal reflects His glory and brings Him ultimate honor (John 17). This is the beauty of evangelism, that God allows creation to be both recipients and participants in His redemptive plan.

But how do we know if we're doing it right?

Success in Evangelism

God's Role: John 6:44 says it like this, "No one can come to me unless the Father who sent me draws him, and I will raise him up at the last day." Not only does God have to draw the person, but also every person that is drawn to God must experience a spiritual rebirth. Jesus tells Nicodemus in John 3, "I tell you the truth, no one can see the kingdom of God unless he is born again." The term "born again" has three important nuances attached to it.

First, it implies to be reborn, to rehappen. The reason why we have to be reborn is because the first birth accompanied spiritual death (Eph 2:1-3). Every person is born spiritually dead and separated from God. Because of sin, a rebirth must occur.

The second implication is that the birth is from above. The word which is translated "again," literally means from above. Therefore, not only must a person be reborn, but also the source of this rebirth can only be God.

The final nuance is that this birth must come from the same one who gave you birth the first time—God. Jesus wants to make it as clear as possible that to be a child of God comes from God.

Our Role: In 1 Corinthians 3:5-9, Paul holds man responsible for two acts in evangelism: planting and watering. In 1 Corinthians 3:6-7, he says, "I planted the seed, Apollos watered it, but God made it grow. So neither he who plants nor he who waters is anything, but only God, who makes things grow." Paul implies that, as God's people, we have an opportunity to assist our great king in kingdom work, but it is clear that we only play a supporting role. Just as in harvesting a crop, a person's role in evangelism is as follows:

We start with a seed, which is the gospel. Paul says that we are then given the opportunity to plant this seed in the hearts of men. Planting happens whenever we share the Gospel. Watering is the next step. The scriptures do not speak specifically about what watering appears to be. However, we can conclude that Paul is implying that any work motivated by the love of God that is used to benefit the Gospel, is, in all practical purposes, "watering." After watering, man's role is finished and it is only up to God to give someone life.

The Joy of Participating

Paul affirms the importance of our role in God's agenda to bring people to Him. But the responsibility to produce spiritual life belongs only to God.

It is impossible for any person to make someone a follower of Christ. No one can be talked into salvation. We can't pray hard enough, love radically enough, give generously enough, and persuade convincingly enough to make someone give his or her life to Christ. There is nothing we can do to produce spiritual life in ourselves or another person. Only Jesus possesses that ability and authority.

Having the knowledge that God has to supernaturally stir within someone the desire to worship Christ takes the pressure off of us. This reality also implies a definition of success that is unlike natural man. Man determines success by productivity. God determines success by faithfulness. Although we cannot produce faith, through the power of the Holy Spirit, we can be obedient. God doesn't ask us to save anyone or talk anyone into worshipping Him. He only asks that we experience the joy of proclaiming the good news (Acts 20:24ff). Therefore, an appropriate definition for evangelism, which I have humbly paraphrased from the great leader Bill Bright, is this: **Go into the world, empowered by the Spirit and motivated by Christ's love, to share the gospel with all people and trust God with the results.**[3]

Results Driven Evangelism

There is great danger in evangelizing for results rather than out of obedience and honor for God.

First, results-driven evangelism implies that we actually play a part in spiritual rebirth. This is harmful thinking that gives people and their actions credit when all glory should go to God.

Second, it puts undue pressure on God's people. When we focus on results, we gauge our evangelism experience as good or bad based on the response of those being evangelized. If we go out and share our faith with a results-driven mentality and people don't come to Christ, we'll feel inadequate. This belief could diminish our desire to evangelize, which is destructive to our spiritual growth and stewardship.

Another danger is the tendency to change the message. When I was a student at Miami University, I wanted people to come to Christ so much that when I shared the Gospel, I wouldn't even bring up repentance. I would forget to tell people that they would have to change their lives if they accepted Christ because it might scare them off. Looking back, I didn't intentionally or maliciously leave repentance out; it was a subconscious reaction to my desire to yield results. Sadly, my aspiration to be successful in the eyes of man drove me to preach false doctrine. I wasn't focusing on faithfulness, but productivity.

If we are driven by results, then how well we do is no longer based on God's word, but on how the hearer responds to the message. 2 Corinthians 2:15-16 says that, "For we are to God the aroma of Christ among those who are being saved and those who are perishing. To the one we are the smell of death; to the other, the fragrance of life..." Paul gives us the realistic picture of what life in Christ looks like. He says that those who are believers are like an aroma to the world. To those who want to love God, we are a beautiful, desirous fragrance. To those who do not believe, we smell like death. If we are not convinced that the Gospel is inherently offensive, we will try to do whatever it takes to allow the hearer to be most comfortable. Some might ask, "Do we then have no responsibility?" Yes we do! Remember, we are to plant and water. Our responsibility is to share the gospel in love (1 Cor. 2:1).

MAJOR ON THE PRINCIPLES

Although there is debate on how to practically minister to others, there should be no debate on clear biblical principles pertaining to ministry and our role as God's children. Feel free to implement whatever method seems prudent to your situation. However, we must not argue over a few clear principles that Jesus demonstrated in His life and ministry.

Intentionality: Being intentional requires honesty. We must admit that seldom does one share his or her faith by default. God gives us the mandate to proclaim Him because the default mode of the world is idol worship, not Christ worship. If we do not actively engage our world about Jesus, the default mode is to never discuss Him. Make no mistake, intentionality is assumed by Jesus, as noted throughout his exhortations in the New Testament (i.e. Mt. 10:5-10ff). We must be intentional in our personal evangelism and intentionality must be a key component when we train others in evangelism.

Biblical Holistic Conviction: We must ensure that those under our care will be intentionally developed in the biblical understanding of service and evangelism.

Strive to ensure that neither you nor those you train are confined to one specific style of service and evangelism. Ensure that people are trained based on biblical conviction, rather than personality or preferences. The result is that both you and those you disciple will be equipped to proclaim the gospel in many different scenarios. This isn't done so you can be flashy or versatile, but rather so that you may be who God created you to be: One who is ready to proclaim Jesus anywhere and to anyone.

Transferable: Jesus models that transferability is a must when training or being trained in ministry (Jn 4:1-2; Lk 10:1-16ff). We must teach those who are being discipled how to grow in the area of service and evangelism in order that they will eventually be able to teach others.

Jesus never asked anyone to do or be anything which first He had not demonstrated in His own life. His desire was to get the disciples into a vital experience with God. It is important that we realize that these early disciples really did not do much other than watch Jesus for at least a year before He began to implore them to minister to others. However, the vision was kept before them by His activity that eventually they would reproduce what they had seen and heard. The model has been set for us. The mission of equipping in order to be able to communicate our faith to the world through ministry (service and evangelism) was a huge element of discipleship in Jesus' approach.

Hopefully, you have seen how the word and ministry are integral to making disciples. Next, we will discuss the third piece of the puzzle – relationship.

RELATIONSHIP IN DISCIPLESHIP

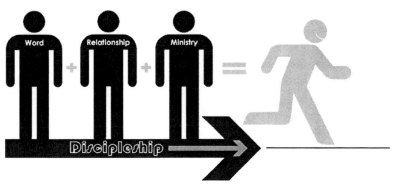

A ll aspects of discipleship are important, but relationship is the element that provides the platform for word and ministry. It's fitting that the glue to successful discipleship is not stated in a theological treaty but is clearly seen through practical demonstration. I mention this because there is no explicit mandate given in the Bible that you must develop a relationship with people in order to build them up in their Christian faith. However, what is obvious through Christ's display is that after calling His men, He made a practice of being with them. This was the nature of his training program — letting his disciples follow him as he did life and ministry. The knowledge of Christ was gained by association, while it was understood by explanation (Lk. 8:10). He ate with His disciples, slept next to them, and talked with them. Let's take a look at a few examples.

Matthew 13:10-12
¹⁰The disciples came to him and asked, "Why do you speak to the people in parables?" ¹¹He replied, "The knowledge of the secrets of the kingdom of heaven has been given to you, but not to them. ¹²Whoever has will be given more, and he will have an abundance. Whoever does not have, even what he has will be taken from him.

John 11:54
Therefore Jesus no longer moved about publicly among the Jews. Instead he withdrew to a region near the desert, to a village called Ephraim, where he stayed with his disciples.

Matthew 9:9

As Jesus went on from there, he saw a man named Matthew sitting at the tax collector's booth. "Follow me," he told him, and Matthew got up and followed him.

Luke 22:39-41

[39]Jesus went out as usual to the Mount of Olives, and his disciples followed him. [40]On reaching the place, he said to them, "Pray that you will not fall into temptation." [41]He withdrew about a stone's throw beyond them, knelt down and prayed

Jesus accomplished the task of developing His disciples by growing their friendship, which allowed them to build trust and confidence in His leadership. So, how do you build a relationship that makes discipleship seamless and obtainable?

THE IMPORTANCE OF INTENTIONALITY

Have you ever heard Christians describe how they were "like Jesus" by not having an agenda when interacting with others? They are implying that Jesus was unintentional in what He did, that He interacted without purpose, particularly in his discipleship. This is false. In fact, there has never been a more intentional, calculated plan in history than the discipleship ministry of Jesus.

The danger in this 'no agenda' remark is that many Christians actually believe it – that to truly love someone you should have no agenda. Although Jesus loved unconditionally, He didn't love without an agenda. To love someone with an agenda is to love someone with a plan of things to be done. It would be hard to disagree that Jesus had a temporally-organized plan for matters to be attended to before His crucifixion.

Everything Jesus did was calculated in order to maximize glory for the Father. We witness Jesus clearly expressing his agenda in Matthew 16:23-28, revealing that He knew what His goal was and that nothing was going to deter Him. Was the one who defines love not loving, simply because He had a plan?

Jesus was no less strategic when it came to how He treated His disciples. His love was always unconditional, while at the same time, He always had a goal: for His disciples to be servants of God that would eventually reproduce their lives in others. Jesus wanted them to be developed in order to develop others, on how to walk by faith, communicate their faith, and multiply their faith.

The intentionality of how He ministered to the disciples is further proof of His strategic focus. He chose them out of a crowd in order for them to realize they were part of His inner circle. He wanted to be closer to them than He was to the masses. He taught them things that He had not taught others. He was especially vulnerable with them. He trusted them with information to which nobody else was privy.

Jesus made building relationships with the disciples a priority, rather than merely connecting with them when He had the opportunity. The former shows commitment; the latter communicates indifference.

In every situation, Jesus' deeds were done for specific reasons: He did only what the Father commanded. Although there is no direct exhortation for the laymen to commit to such a level when speaking about relationships, it seems convincing that Jesus shows us how important the developing of the relationship is to growing a disciple in Christ.

Christ's model, coupled with His exhortation to obey, shows that those who follow Christ will be developing relationships with others for the purpose of spiritual multiplication.

THE IMPORTANCE OF COMMITMENT

It's difficult to share our joys, struggles, fears, and pain with someone when we don't even know how long they will be around or how much they care. Vulnerability and accountability are hard to have if you are not sure the other person is committed to you. Commitment is something that we don't like to talk about much because it takes work and patience – things we unfairly label as rigid and absent-hearted.

Commitment is the bridge to intimacy. You may be in a discipleship relationship with someone who isn't your best buddy, someone who has different interests and passions. But, you're both committed to Jesus and to each other. When you live in commitment to one another, friendship and intimacy often follow. We cannot put the cart before the horse.

If you're "not feeling" your discipleship time because you're paired with someone who you're not super close with, just be patient. When your discipler is committed to serving you, journeying with you, and you are both focused on Christ, intimacy will develop. Commitment is the string that holds together love as a decision and love as intimacy. We all want to be loved and cared for, but without commitment, these things will never occur.

Intentionality and commitment provide an atmosphere that allows relationships to flourish. These are the main non-negotiables that commitment breeds: authenticity, vulnerability, longevity and accountability.

Authenticity

Authenticity is realness. It is the absence of fake, to be truly who we are. Very few of us possess the ability to be completely honest and forthright upon meeting someone for the first time. We often need time to build trust and make sure the other person is committed to us before we share our hearts. Our honesty level usually increases as relationship safety increases. The more dependable and committed our friend is, the easier it is for us to be authentic.

Authenticity is key for a healthy discipleship relationship. If a relationship isn't authentic, then it is disingenuous and loses its redemptive potential. Without authenticity, our true hearts are never fully brought into light.

Vulnerability

We often mistake vulnerability and authenticity as interchangeable ideas. We can be honest with someone without being vulnerable, able to restate the facts but unable or unwilling to share how the facts make us feel. This is where vulnerability finds its home.

Being vulnerable is never about the restatement of facts; it's about letting people into the heart and emotions of the situations that transpire in your life. Vulnerability allows people to see that you are human. This is where true intimacy begins, when you stop being the only person that knows your heart by letting others into it.

Longevity

Along with commitment comes longevity. In our culture, to commit to something is scary, but to commit to something with longevity is outright lunacy. From private sector businesses to professional sports, it's unorthodox to stay somewhere and plant roots. Seldom do we want to commit ourselves with a time attachment; we want to know where the back door is. Longevity seems scary because it requires us to loosen our selfish grip on two things: our time and mobility. We regard our time and mobility as treasure when we should be committed to the cause of Christ.

In contrast, God's commitment to his people is not seasonal or circumstantial; it is eternal. Jesus didn't hang out with His disciples and bail after He taught them some stuff. He stayed with them, labored with them, fought with them. He modeled longevity, which in turn built security within the relationship. Jesus was committed and the disciples knew it because He put in the hours. Longevity in discipleship relationships is essential.

Accountability

Accountability is almost a nonexistent concept in the Christian community today, but it was – and is – foundational to Jesus' ministry. Let me show you an example in scripture:

Deuteronomy 23:14
For the LORD your God moves about in your camp to protect you and to deliver your enemies to you. Your camp must be holy, so that he will not see among you anything indecent and turn away from you.

1 Corinthians 5:9-13
[9]I have written you in my letter not to associate with sexually immoral people—
[10]not at all meaning the people of this world who are immoral, or the greedy and swindlers, or idolaters. In that case you would have to leave this world. [11]But now I am writing you that you must not associate with anyone who calls himself a brother but is sexually immoral or greedy, an idolater or a slanderer, a drunkard or a swindler. With such a man do not even eat. [12]What business is it

of mine to judge those outside the church? Are you not to judge those inside? [13]God will judge those outside. "Expel the wicked man from among you."

These verses address the concept of keeping holiness in the camp. God called His people to be set apart so that they might demonstrate to the world what it looks like to serve the living God by bearing His image well. In doing so, the Lord would bless His people so that those who were spectators would then desire to serve Him.

Whenever Israelites within the camp fell into sin, God would stop blessing and protecting them, call the community to cleanse the camp, find out who is in sin, and eradicate it so as to not taint the whole camp.

Here we see that holiness was important to the Father, and therefore, it should be important to us. This is where accountability finds its expression. It is not about sinning and being reprimanded for it. Accountability is about those in the family of God spurring one another on toward love and good in Jesus. It is a purposeful exchange to see people move closer to Christ-likeness.

Does this change the awkwardness and difficulty of calling out sin? No. Does this make it any easier or comfortable to ask our fellow brothers and sisters the hard questions necessary for exposing and fighting sin? Absolutely not. What it does is allow us to keep our journey in Christ in the light. It allows holiness to be a joy, not just an option. It provides opportunity to build deep, intimate friendships and show the world a clearer picture of Jesus.

Being accountable to God and His people allows us to know our sin and be intent on dealing with it. The goal of accountability is intimacy with Jesus, which then provides intimacy with each other.

Commitment and all it encompasses – authenticity, vulnerability, longevity, and accountability – will pave the way to an intimate and holistic discipleship relationship.

THE IMPORTANCE OF LOVE

Imagine Jesus teaching scripture to the disciples, sitting each one down and instructing them on how to share the gospel, but as soon as the lesson is over, He leaves. Isn't that a weird image?

He didn't just teach his disciples but nurtured their friendship. He made them feel like people instead of projects.

I once felt like a project. The Christian group with which I was involved in college connected me with a student leader, and I must confess that I resented him. He always wondered why we didn't connect. It was partially because of my own lack of integrity; it was easy for me to have an excuse to not be faithful to him and the group I was a part of. But also, I never really felt valued for simply being "Eric." Whenever he wanted to meet, it was to train me to do something, either to study the Bible or share my faith. He rarely wanted to talk about how my life was going. Our interactions led me to distrust his intentions and feel cold toward him, and so our friendship was short-lived. He showed commitment and intentionality, but not genuine love.

We never earned God's love. He created us and then decided to love us. In the same way, we should love the person we are in a discipleship relationship with simply because he is our brother, not because he's cool or we get along well. As 1 John 4:19 says, "We love because He first loved us."

Love "based on decision" provides the opportunity for love "based on intimacy" to develop. Love gives us the freedom and safety to be interdependent with someone. Love creates the desire to have consistent interactions. Love allows safety and room to build healthy emotional attachment.

Needless to say, love is central to us as created beings. We as people have a universal need to belong and to love, which is satisfied when an intimate relationship is formed.

Love is the motivation behind healthy relationships. It is what produces commitment and intentionality. It is a nonnegotiable that the person being discipled should not only know he or she is loved by Christ, but also by those who desire to train him or her.

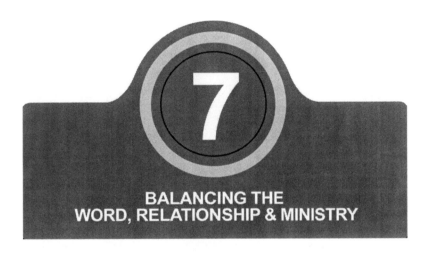

BALANCING THE
WORD, RELATIONSHIP & MINISTRY

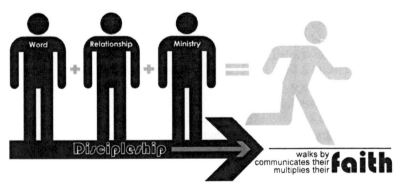

AIMING FOR EQUILIBRIUM

The danger within any ministry is an unbalanced state in one's spiritual development. Churches may desire to be competent in all three areas, but they often find themselves streamlining their energy into just one or two. Also, imbalance might manifest itself more covertly – a ministry might think it has some areas down pat, but it really isn't following through on them as fully as it should.

One church I used to serve with had very good teachers: men and women faithfully and effectively trained their church body in the scriptures and were constantly referring to the word. In ministry, however, the church was lacking. The people weren't being trained in how to personally share their faith. They weren't equipped on how to be bold in evangelism. Their service consisted of occasionally visiting a soup kitchen.

A different church I have been with boasted a very strong relationship component. Church members were hanging out together, being vulnerable and holding each other accountable. When it came to studying the Bible, however, things were shaky. Laymen weren't being trained on how to adequately read the scriptures. In fact, it wasn't strange if a Bible study group didn't teach the Bible.

Do you see the imbalance that exists between the discipleship components of these two churches? In both cases, the concern is not the total disregard of Christ's commands, but rather not allowing the full measure of what Christ desired to be evident through the life of the church.

We must be intentional about developing ministries that allow us to peek into Christ's heart and make sure that His desires are fully satisfied in our devotion to Him.

The Result of Imbalance

To neglect any component of word, relationship, and ministry is irresponsible discipleship. Instruction (word) without intimacy (relationship) produces dispassionate robots. Teaching (word) coupled with a vibrant friendship (relationship) but void of service (ministry), produces spiritually constipated Christians—people who only receive but don't give out. Strong, brotherly bonds (relationship) that eschew any teaching (word) and evangelism (ministry) produce shallow and disobedient Christians.

The Lord modeled depth in Relationship, the Word, and Ministry. Through the power of the Holy Spirit, he produced holistic and healthy followers. We have been given the privilege and the mandate to do likewise.

THE GOAL OF WORD, RELATIONSHIP, AND MINISTRY

The beauty of human worship is unlike anything else in creation — it is intelligent and deliberate. Stars worship God by being stars, and mountains worship God by being mountains. However, God has given humans the unique capacity to assert their volition. We have the ability of choosing to worship God or not.

Even though you have that choice, the reason you're here is to be who Jesus created you to be and to do what Jesus has created you to do. The reason we train disciples in word, relationship, and ministry is to place them in an atmosphere where they can fulfill Jesus' plan for them. Jesus' desire for every believer is perhaps best expressed in Romans 12:1.

Therefore, I urge you, brothers, in view of God's mercy,
to offer your bodies as living sacrifices, holy and pleasing
to God—this is your spiritual act of worship.

As a "living sacrifice," we reflect a permanent and perpetual offering, an intelligent and deliberate sacrifice to God. He desires all of whom we are – our temperament, personality, sexuality, etc. – to be given to Him continually. God wants us to choose Jesus intentionally, moment by moment.

Word, relationship, and ministry are not ends in themselves. They are the means by which we create an environment that fosters an individual's growth in Christ. They are the tools we use to position ourselves to live lives of perpetual worship that are glorifying to God. The goal of Word, Relationship and Ministry is this: that disciples will walk by faith, communicate their faith, and multiply their faith.

Walking by Faith

There is no such thing as a non-walking Christian. Walking, in essence, means living. It is the whole manner of a person's life and conduct. Particularly in the New Testament, "walking," when used metaphorically, indicates a studied observance of a new rule of life. This new life is characteristic of believers and is in contrast to their "walk" in their unregenerate days. Let's look at what Jesus said in Matthew 7:19-27:

[19]Every tree that does not bear good fruit is cut down and thrown into the fire. [20]Thus, by their fruit you will recognize them. [21]"Not everyone who says to me, 'Lord, Lord,' will enter the kingdom of heaven, but only he who does the will of my Father who is in heaven. [22]Many will say to me on that day, 'Lord, Lord, did we not prophesy in your name, and in your name drive out demons and perform many miracles?' [23]Then I will tell them plainly, 'I never knew you. Away from me, you evildoers!' [24]"Therefore everyone who hears these words of mine and puts them into practice is like a wise man who built his house on the rock. [25]The rain came down, the streams rose, and the winds blew and beat against that house; yet it did not fall, because it had its foundation on the rock. [26]But everyone who hears these words of mine and does not put them into practice is like a foolish man who built his house on sand. [27]The rain came down, the streams rose, and the winds blew and beat against that house, and it fell with a great crash."

In his sermon, Jesus presents a contrast between the genuine Christian and the fake Christian. One professes, the other truly believes and obeys. The one who professes may deceive men, even himself, but will not deceive God, and the one who truly believes and obeys will be recognized by his or her fruit. Christians (people who walk by faith) are to obey the Sermon on the Mount, not merely admire it.

Walking by faith is the continual demonstration of one's shift from their old life under ownership of self and Satan to their new life under ownership of God.

In all, a disciple of Christ is involved in the body of Christ through study, worship, prayer, service, witnessing, and the stewardship of one's time, talent, and treasure.

Communicating Their Faith

Ministry is often mistakenly seen as a task that needs to be accomplished. But in reality, Jesus wants ministry to be a lifestyle. God expects all believers to be His messengers in sharing the Gospel with the unbelieving world. For Jesus, ministry was paramount to following Him. There is not a single person in scripture that heard a message from Jesus and was not called to proclaim the good news to others. The body of Christ has a mandate to protect the theological integrity of our message (1 Tim. 4:16) and to proclaim the truth to the world.

Every day presents numerous opportunities for us to tell the story of Jesus in our spheres of influence. Sadly, we often choose not to take advantage of these opportunities. We may have a desire to share our faith, but we usually don't, either because we don't know how or because we're afraid.

Like Jesus did with his disciples, we need to first model ministry before we ask our disciples to do it. Have your disciple watch you share your faith with people. Let them ask questions and coach them up. Whether it be engaging random strangers on the street or strategically initiating conversations with family members or co-workers, remember that ministry is a spiritual discipline that will not strengthen without intentionality. A disciple is one who witnesses for Christ as a way of life (Matthew 5:16) through service and evangelism.

Multiplying Their Faith

Implicit in the command "Make Disciples" is that when we train a person to walk by faith and communicate their faith, they are in turn expected to multiply their faith. As you train your disciples, they should reach a level of maturity where they can make disciples on their own.

Hopefully, it has been made clear that the Bible teaches that a true disciple's heart is bent toward making other disciples. We are to take a cue from Paul when he told Timothy to take the good news and entrust it with reliable men who will then in turn teach others.

According to Christ's commission, we make a disciple by initiating them into the family of God and then teaching them to obey all that Jesus commanded. So, the inferred progression is as follows: Just as Person A is teaching Person B to obey all that Jesus commanded, our Lord commands Person B to make disciples and teach them all He commanded, and so on. This is spiritual multiplication. Let's take a look at how Jesus communicated this concept to his disciples:

John 21:15
When they had finished eating, Jesus said to Simon Peter,
"Simon son of John, do you truly love me more than these?"
"Yes, Lord," he said, "you know that I love you." Jesus said, "Feed my lambs."

Matthew 4:19; Mark 1:17
"Come, follow me," Jesus said, "and I will make you fishers of men."

John 20:21
Again Jesus said, "Peace be with you! As the Father has sent me, I am sending you."

When Jesus tells us to be shepherds of sheep and fishers of men, He's calling us to be missionaries that will make disciples. The individuals we disciple should understand this call, and we must make it clear that one of the main reasons we are pouring into them is so they can soon pour into others for Jesus' glory.

With an environment that allows word, relationship, and ministry to flourish, the promise that people have an opportunity to intentionally be taught how to walk by faith, communicate their faith and multiply their faith, is where holistic discipleship finds its fulfillment. This allows us to finally have metrics to base our faithfulness (or lack thereof) on, because discipleship is finally defined.

PART II

Man's Method

INTRODUCING DISCIPLESHIP

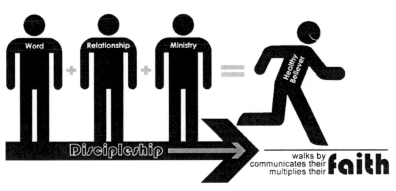

Word + Relationship + Ministry = Healthy Believer

Discipleship

walks by
communicates their
multiplies their **faith**

I t would be unwise of me to champion one specific, strict method of faithful discipleship to which all churches and individuals must adhere. What has been discussed thus far are the non-negotiables of discipleship, the theological framework needed to build a Gospel-centered method, spared of any opinions or preferences. As long as you hold close the biblical principles of discipleship and proceed faithfully, I want to encourage you to roll with the flavor or rhythm that fits best. There are many ways to disciple a person or build a ministry that are faithful to Christ's mandate of discipleship.

During this portion of the book, I want individuals and organizations alike to be able to take practical next steps in being faithful to Jesus' command of making disciples. My hope is that through presenting these ideas you would be encouraged to put God's clear principles into practice.

Again, we are discussing methods to use in order to see clear principles put into practice. The goal is that readers will use this dialogue in the ongoing discussion of discipleship as a springboard to implement other creative ways of carrying out Biblical principles in a holistic manner.

Please add to, subtract from, or tweak according to the style for which your situation calls. The only thing we insist on is that you treat the elements discussed in the first portion of the book as principles and not preferences. In fact, spend considerable time building conviction from God's principles before thinking through practical implementation methods.

Just some methods!

BEFORE YOU BEGIN DISCIPLESHIP...

Prepare Your Heart

The question for our churches is not, "Are we discipling?" But, "Are we discipling holistically?" This question has the potential to rock some boats, because the answer may imply that some are not serving Christ faithfully in their church. After all, who wants to be guilty of not being a faithful servant of God? However, critique on the church (with the goal of seeing us fulfill our potential in Christ) shouldn't be taken as a personal attack on the character and hearts of the leaders and the body. While the question at hand may indict some people, the majority of churches have good hearts and pure, Christ-honoring motives. The desired conclusion from such a question is that God will reveal where we miss the mark and compel us to humble ourselves and change in order to honor him best.

Be Honest With Your Present Situation

Whenever I ask a church or a Christian if they are doing discipleship, it's the individual that is usually much more humble and willing to say "no" and even ask for help. The different church leaders unanimously have said, "Yes," and then they spend a few minutes explaining aspects of their ministry in order to reveal areas where people are being trained in their church. I think the issue is a fundamental difference in thinking. I am not concerned with the fact that a few people in a church are making disciples. It seems that Jesus' concern is this: We are not providing a DNA where the heart of what we do is making disciples.

The church leader will hardly ever ask for help, but at the end of the conversation they will casually slip in, "Do you have any thoughts on what we can do?" The reality is that the majority of Christians are not being intentionally and holistically developed, and for some reason or another, leaders are usually unwilling to admit it.

In regard to the individual, realizing his or her need to "make disciples" is the most important step toward faithfulness in Christ. But with churches, the difficulty in such a conversation is that it becomes very hard to implement change. To change something means that the leaders have to admit that something is wrong. Or even more drastic, if there are no aspects of discipleship happening, then change might mean restructuring the ministry.

I will be the first to admit that it is hard for us to see areas of shortcoming and acknowledge them readily. At first, people I have encountered will resist the fact that discipleship is an area that they could do in a healthier way. But eventually, every person that I have approached about discipleship wants change. So does change happen? Almost never. Why not?

Every time I was asked to help a church become more discipleship-driven, I was also met with resistance. The reason for the opposition was never because the leader did not think the change was biblical. One hundred percent of the time, the reason was simple pragmatics. They simply did not think it would work. The leader was concerned that people would leave their church and not step up to the commitment that discipleship requires. The leaders would rather continue doing what was normal and safe than challenge people, rock the boat, risk people leaving their church, even if it meant leading people exactly where Christ wants them – into a relationship where believing the Gospel actually costs the person something.

On the other hand, I see people using components of discipleship within their ministry because it will be practically beneficial. It's dangerous when our pragmatism guides our theology and not the other way around. Theology, not pragmatism, should be a reason for change. Hopefully, we are biblically convicted that making disciples is what God has called us to. Equally, I hope you are convinced that Jesus defines what that should look like.

If your church really longs for change, it had better be grounded on something more than just wanting to shake things up or desiring a new change of scenery. If you want to implement discipleship or take it more seriously, it needs to be because you buy into what Jesus is saying. You must crave change for the single reason that Jesus provided a clear standard of what it means to equip individuals to be the people of God.

Know What You're Getting Into

It's good to know what you're getting into. What the process of discipleship will do is eliminate the enormous middle ground of lukewarm "believers" who call themselves Christians but don't live as if Jesus is their king. It weeds out those who don't want to walk with the Lord and allows those who do to step up. Discipleship doesn't ask people to be super-Christians, just regular ones. If people are hesitant to enter into the discipleship process that you and/or leadership has implemented, it could very well be revealing their heart.

If you agree with me that discipleship is extremely biblical and that it is what Christ wants of your ministry, then I pray that you implement it. You may be worrying about the numbers. People might not come through the doors in droves. Finances might become an issue. You could be concerned about hanging onto your church building. But let me ask you, are you more concerned with what man thinks or with what God thinks?

If we look at Jesus' ministry, we'll see that He spoke to large crowds, but intentionally got intimate with a few. He made the crowd choose if they were going to be in or out. Jesus was willing to turn off the masses to train a few disciples to reach the world.

Rethink Ministry – "Own the Vision"

Owning the vision versus renting the vision is an idiom introduced from the perspective that you are more dedicated to something that you own opposed to something that you rent.

Have you ever driven a leased car? Even if you're normally a responsible, perhaps even a cautious person, the fact that it's not *really* yours makes you a bit more lenient with it. You might carelessly juggle a mug of coffee while you drive, abstain from washing the car's exterior, or not even flinch if your child's basketball smacks up against its side. But if you owned the same car, think about how much more attention you'd pay to it. You'd probably take it to the car wash once in a while and avoid spilling on the seats or denting the doors. Because you assume ownership, you feel compelled to take care of it and see the car through. It's the same way in ministry. If you cast a vision, but don't own it, it's probably not going to work.

When you own a vision, you cannot even think that it might not work. If you own the vision, you operate from a perspective not of, "Will this happen?" but, "When will this happen?" People who own a vision get behind it with all they have.

When we use vernacular like "owning a vision," people usually think of business ventures. However, all of us own visions every day — we just may not realize it.

For example, how many churches in America consider whether they should have some sort of ministry for their youth? I think it is safe to say probably not many. Not many churches or people attending churches are considering having some type of ministry to the youth. It is assumed. Why do we make that assumption? Because without thinking, engrained in us is a belief (and rightfully so) that you do whatever you need to do in order to make sure that our youth are placed in an environment to learn about Jesus. The church may not know exactly how to structure their youth ministry, they may not know who will run it or where they will hold it, but they are convicted that they need it. Obstacles won't prevent them from reaching their goal of having a youth ministry. They own the vision.

When you come into a situation owning a vision, all doubts and questions about the vision must be viewed as opportunities to make the vision stronger, not as threats to disband it.

Renting a vision is, at its core, different from owning a vision. The difference is the undergirding belief system. Individuals with a renter mindset are more likely to be indifferent to the success of the idea. Notice indifference is not that they don't like the idea but that there is no conviction. Without conviction, how do you outlast times of doubt?

If you have a renter's mindset, your commitment may wax and wane, and you'll be susceptible to disengaging from the goal when things are scrutinized. Renters are like fair weather friends and will take credit for the wins. However, when it's all on the line, they are less likely to roll with the punches and will not go down with the ship. Ideas formed from people with this kind of mindset hardly ever make it out of the boardroom.

When we present all the obstacles of an idea without first owning the vision, we actually prevent ourselves from owning the vision and end up killing it. I spend ample time on this subject because I find it to be the bottleneck that hinders radical change in individuals and churches. I know many people who get excited about "making disciples" and are very well intentioned, but they don't spend time to make it a conviction-level belief; they never really own this vision, and eventually the emotion and excitement fade.

Implementing discipleship in one's life or in one's church is extremely difficult if you are not convinced that it's not just a suggestion from a pastor, but a command from God.

There are many appropriate questions that need to be addressed when thinking about discipleship: What steps do you take to move people coming to your church for the first time to be comfortable and not feel out of place because they are not in a discipleship relationship? What if the wife wants to be discipled but the husband doesn't? What if a family is too busy for your process? What if I do not want to disciple the person given to me because we don't connect well? Before any of these questions are answered, it is vital that the individuals asking the questions have already understood and owned the vision of discipleship.

If you are leading a ministry, it is important that you align other leaders or staff team members with the vision of discipleship in its theological and practical intricacies. After people are on board theologically with what it means to disciple, then the logical question to ask the team is, "Are the things we have learned about discipleship happening in our lives and in our local sphere?" It is important that this question is answered by analyzing the ministry through tangible measures in order to have an assessment of the ministry as unbiased as possible.

If the answer is that we are not practicing holistic discipleship, then we must ask, "What is our reasoning behind not pursuing it?" At this point, the goal is to get your leaders on board in wanting to see discipleship flourishing in their local ministry. It is important that the team recognizes the need before presenting the vision for holistic discipleship.

Once our thinking is shaped, our hearts are prepared, and we own the vision, we are ready for the journey that obeying Christ's mandate will take us on.

DISCIPLESHIP STEP BY STEP

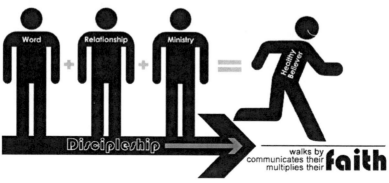

N ow that we've defined discipleship as well as prepared our heart and mind, let's talk about the nuts and bolts. How do we practically start taking steps to have discipleship be a lifestyle and not just doctrine with which we agree? Here, I've provided a brief glimpse at the steps we've taken in implementing discipleship at Mack Avenue Community Church.

Again, it's not about the process but a faithful application of the principles that they encapsulate.

STEP 1: IT ALL STARTS WITH THE LEADERSHIP

My friend Ken came to Christ in his early twenties, and almost immediately, the Lord used him to start a Bible study. The study quickly grew to thirty people under Ken's leadership. Once when we had lunch together I asked him, "What will happen to this ministry if you leave?" He was confused by my question. I expressed to him my concern that if he left the next day, the ministry would die. He hadn't been discipling men and growing them in Christ, so there was nobody to potentially step up in a leadership position if Ken were to leave. He understood my point and even vowed to disciple some men. Unfortunately, Ken never intentionally trained or developed the men in the study, and after he moved to Chicago three months later, it only took two weeks for the ministry to die.

The theological premise of making disciples is useless if not accompanied by intentional practice. Teaching about biblical discipleship is extremely important, but it must be continually reinforced by the life of a discipler. People learn theological truths when they see them consistently lived out in someone's life. A danger for us as leaders is to understand the theory and ask others to carry out the practice. It is difficult to achieve Holistic discipleship this way. It seems most realistic for a church or organization to produce capable disciplers when its leaders have modeled discipleship for them. Simply, discipleship will happen when they have been discipled. The leadership should be the first to disciple individuals in your church, and they must continue to model discipleship, or the ministry will eventually slide back into its old groove.

When we were first starting out at Mack Ave, we made sure that we were all being discipled. Our staff men and wives committed to meeting weekly where we'd build conviction about the very areas mentioned in chapters 1-6. As time went on, God gave us favor and a few godly leaders. More and more individuals wanted to plug into Mack Ave, which meant they wanted to be discipled.

This step is non-negotiable, because modeling is of utmost importance. Many times I have trained church leaders about discipleship, but *never* has training alone allowed the process of discipleship to be faithfully carried out. If discipleship is truly desired, the method of seeing it commence cannot only consist of a training seminar, a sermon series, or by reading this book. Discipleship won't work unless there is intentional modeling of discipleship. If the leaders are not leading Bible studies, sharing their faith with others, and training people in the faith, then those that are following will eventually follow their lead and likewise refrain from training others. The way people learn discipleship is by seeing it modeled before them. The leadership must actively disciple others in order for those they are leading to know how to disciple. Discipleship is caught, not taught.

STEP 2: SETTING THE FOUNDATION WITH DISCIPLERS

The process of finding the right people and training them is foundational to discipleship. In order to find the right people, we need to take inventory of the church by asking three questions:

Who are the members that are currently serving?
Where are these members currently serving?
Who are the members that are not currently serving?

This is a quick way to discover untapped resources. When a church adopts the biblical philosophy that service is everybody's business, then it is on track to being healthy. It is vital for the precedence to be set that the church is not begging for disciplers, nor is discipleship an optional activity; discipleship has to be seen as organic to how your life and church function. With this mindset, people will understand the significance and responsibility of such a task as being involved in discipleship.

To accept the opportunity of discipling requires a willingness to be trained to disciple correctly. Without proper training, people will falter. If volunteers are treated as a means to an end, without personal consideration, it will affect their motivation. For that reason, the training should allow time for the discipler to grow in competency. In addition, he or she should be able to recognize the church's commitment to invest in them. This is important because we never want to give the misperception that discipleship involves using people as a means to an end. On the contrary, we are to care about each individual's development in Christ; seeing him or her developing others is a by-product, not the focus.

Just as there was a heritage of disciples who originated through Paul's ministry, so also our desire is to see that same lineage become the hallmark of the church. Discipleship in the church should be a continual process in which faithful discipleship would lead to faithful disciples who bring the Gospel to the world.

Although circumstances are not the same as in Jesus' day, Christ modeled the principle that selection is key to discipleship. Jesus demonstrated that the multitudes could be won over if they are given Spirit-filled leaders to follow (Mt. 9:35-38).

It would be of great help if we possessed the omniscience of Jesus. But we don't. Therefore, we have to be as discerning as we can in order to make sure that, like Paul following the model of Jesus, we too choose disciples who will not waste our time and effort, but who will be faithful stewards to what has been entrusted to them (2Tim 2:2).

There are three main criteria that should be under review whenever choosing initial disciplers and future disciples. The persons should be Faithful, Available, and Teachable (**F.A.T.**).

Faithful: This is a person who is worthy of trust. You want to believe that this person will do what he or she says. You want to ensure that what you are entrusting to the person will be in good hands.

Available: This person is obtainable; they are capable of being developed and used. It is hard to impart something to someone who is hard to find. Therefore, the person must show a willingness to want to be around you and the others you are training. He or she must model commitment through attendance.

Teachable: This person allows others to impart knowledge or skill to his or her life. They are willing to receive exhortation and rebuke when appropriate. They must be eager to learn from the example and experience of others and, most importantly, the Scriptures. It is impossible to teach someone something who knows everything. Just as Jesus modeled, we are not to waste the stewardship of our lives with know-it-alls (Matthew 9:12 and Proverbs 8:13).

Without these three traits, it is difficult to develop someone. While we desire everyone to possess these characteristics, we must spend time in prayer, because the Lord may desire us to take a risk on a person who struggles in one or more of these areas. However, the rule of thumb is to allow these traits to be your guiding measure.

STEP 3: BEGIN WITH A MISSIONAL POSTURE

"Being missional" is just a sexier way of expressing "believing the Gospel." Ministry is really what we are talking about. One of the biggest hurdles for Christians and church leaders alike is figuring out how to build an environment where people are proclaiming the Gospel through evangelism and service.

We would be uninformed as leaders if we thought that this problem of mobilization was because Christians are just not excited about seeing God's kingdom expand. But that's not the case. In my thirteen years of ministry, I have seen an overwhelming number of people that love Jesus and desire to tell others about Him. In fact, I have been a part of many local churches that have members almost begging for an opportunity to serve others for Jesus. So, why does it seem like the body of Christ struggles so much in being missional people? I propose that three major elements are lacking:

1. Training

God's people feel ill-equipped. I have heard so many believers tell me that they want to serve others and proclaim Christ but that they have never seen it modeled. Without training people to minister and talk about Jesus, the default ministry tactic of inviting people to church will be all we're capable of.

Equipping God's people to be missionaries to the world is top priority, and our training needs to communicate that. The more opportunities people get to talk about Jesus, serve, and live Gospel centered lives, the more it will look like the norm, rather than an event.

2. Opportunity

We are fooling ourselves as leaders if we simply acknowledge that there are plenty of opportunities out there to make Jesus known and think that we've done our job. It is true that people only have to go as far as the workplace or the store to be on a mission field, but the reality is that the majority of people don't realize it.

We have to help people see those opportunities by providing an environment where people learn that being God's people on mission is a regular part of life. Instead of waiting for people to create their own opportunities to minister, it seems prudent as leaders to train God's people how to minister and then help to foster opportunities and ideas that would encourage missional living.

At Mack Ave, everyone in our body has the opportunity to serve at one of our Corner Store outreaches. We set up two stores on the corner of our neighborhood streets and sell items of need at greatly reduced prices. While doing so, those we serve fill out a brief survey that lets us learn a little more about them. At the end of this outreach, we take the contact information gathered and give it to the MACC Group that led the outreach, and they are responsible for connecting with those we served.

At just one opportunity of ministry that takes less than two hours, believers have had an opportunity for numerous points of Gospel interaction.

We also encourage our people to live outside their house. It is easy to isolate yourself with your sphere of influence, so we try to be intentional about taking time to know our neighbors and the community around us. We naturally build those relationships through dinners, invitations into our homes and opportunities to serve our neighbors – all avenues to engage them with the Gospel.

Our desire is to provide ample opportunities for people to learn how to engage our culture with the Gospel, train others in ministry, and for each of us to do it as a regular part of life.

3. Accountability

All three of these work in tandem to honor the Lord and aid in producing a missional Christian. However, without accountability, it will be very challenging to build a missional culture. For people to minister out of health and for it to be a lifestyle, there needs to be accountability through three ways:

Modeling

The tendency as leaders is to ask others to do something that we feel we don't have the time to do because we are leading the charge. However, that is antithetical to Jesus' model and practical wisdom. Who would you rather listen to: the guy who *tells you what to do* or the guy who *shows you what to do*? Leaders need to be the first to show how ministry can be done and that it can be done in a healthy manner.

Grace Motivation

We as leaders are to model and prepare an environment that shows we minister out of a grace motivated life, and we minister freely based on the rhythm of each of our lives. People should experience great freedom and grace, and we should assist them in learning what is healthy for them as a person as we learn to live missionally.

There are many people in our body who truly understand Gospel-centered missional living, and yet we don't consistently see them at our outreaches. They have come to realize that our structured outreaches do not determine missionality but encourage it. At the same time, I can present to you several instances where these people are having Gospel interactions and connections with people throughout our community. Isn't that what we want?

I'm excited that there is now a culture where our people don't feel a weird compulsion, judgment or favor for attending or not attending outreaches. We want to model, encourage, and help people understand that being a proclaimer of the Gospel is freeing and not oppressive (Gal. 5:1). It should definitely be done but be done with joy. Let's not forsake the latter for a false sense of the former.

Being Courageous and Gospel-Centered

I've been in friendships where the person knows that I love Jesus, but I let the relationship remain at the place of them admiring my moral compass and personal piety in Christ while the Gospel stays in the shadows.

Conversations about the Gospel don't organically occur too often in our everyday lives, so we bear the responsibility of mustering the courage to bring it up, to give people a chance to say yes to Jesus.

It is very important to have a community hold us accountable to display Gospel-centered courage for Christ. Otherwise, the default mode of having relationships where we do not engage others with the Gospel is too easy to revert to.

There is no debate as to whether Jesus commands us all to live as missional Christians. The question is: how do we allow our churches to be centers that help birth missional Christians? Weekend training programs and motivational speeches don't fulfill what our king desires of us. Jesus doesn't want our organizations to do ministry periodically; he wants his people to be missional.

STEP 4: BUILD AN INFRASTRUCTURE TO ACCOMMODATE GROWTH

If you've assessed your situation and come to realize that you or your ministry hasn't been intentionally making disciples, you've already come a long way by exposing the need. If you want to make it happen, make sure to plan ahead. Imagine the following situation: You have twenty people in your ministry that want to be discipled, but there are only three individuals on hand that can disciple them. There isn't infrastructure in place to accommodate the growth. It may take time and patience, but it's important to build up leaders and faithfully disciple a few individuals before you "open the floodgates."

A "discipleship chain" should be made, so you can orchestrate who will be discipling who. Your 'chart' should give you a big picture visual of who is being discipled, which you should then use to game plan which individuals are ready to disciple, ensuring that no one falls through the cracks of ministry. The discipleship chain and its implementation must start with the leadership. (Please consider your specific church polity when developing your chain). Here I've provided an example of such a chain:

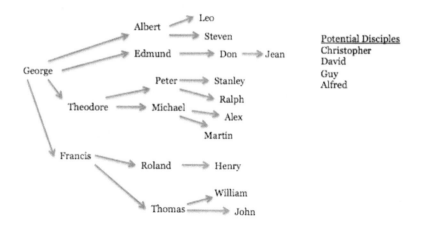

It's important that you don't burn your people out. It is for this reason that I advise putting a maximum capacity on the number of individuals one can disciple. At Mack Ave, if you're not on staff, you can only disciple two people.

In order to gauge whether a person is ready to disciple someone, measure it by humility and maturity, not longevity. It shouldn't matter how long someone has been at your church or how long he or she has been a Christian. It should matter that their character model's F.A.T. and that they possess a passion to walk by faith, communicate their faith and multiply their faith.

I view it as bad stewardship to give a disciple an unhealthy discipler. Even as I'm finishing this book, there are women in our body who want to be discipled, but we don't have the capacity. Those waiting have been gracious and appreciate the fact that we will not place them with women who are not experiencing the spiritual health to disciple. We are hopeful that through love, training, accountability, and by god's grace, women in our body would soon be able to disciple other women.

Be ready to tackle questions of capacity and health when building your model of discipleship. It will communicate great love to your community.

STEP 5: SET CLEAR EXPECTATIONS

Before you start discipling someone, set clear expectations. Tell your disciple the standards to which you will hold them and what their commitment will look like. Tell them how you're going to hold them accountable. When you start things off by setting clear expectations, there's no gray area. Your disciple is either on board or not. There's no room for excuses or dancing around with one foot in and one foot out. That goes for you, too. As the discipler, setting clear expectations means full disclosure. By being clear and straightforward, you are encouraging your disciple that there will be no surprises in their development. You want them to encounter all that Jesus has for them and nothing less.

If you are not willing to be clear about your intentions when discipling, and if you are not intentional about communicating to the person what you desire them to learn, it will be extremely difficult for holistic discipleship to take place.

Along with setting clear expectations, you should be setting the bar high. When you communicate how serious discipleship is, it either causes people to bow out or step up.

At Mack Ave, we simply try to be as clear as possible in order for people to know exactly the cost to be on mission in our community. The requirements of a person interested in discipleship at Mack Ave are:

- Commitment to:
  - Jesus
  - Discipleship (Owns the principles in ch. 1-6)

- Mack Ave Community Church
- Our community (ZIP Code 48214), and the world

- Must desire to be a F.A.T. believer:
  - Faithful
  - Available
  - Teachable

What will your requirements be?

STEP 6: IMPLEMENT THE COMPONENTS

Those discipleship requirements are fulfilled through two components, individual and communal.

One-On-One

Everyone in our community that is being discipled meets intentionally with someone based on their schedules. Some people meet every week, while others meet every two weeks. It's flexible but always consistent.

I currently disciple six men (again - we don't allow anyone who is not on staff to disciple more than two people). Personally, it would be very difficult if I met them individually every week. I meet with them in two groups for training the first week, and the second week I meet with them in two groups for group intimacy (where we share our lives, encourage each other, and have fun). The third week is where I meet with them individually, and we have individual intimacy, and everyone has the final week to rest. The reason we don't make a rigid rule that demands every discipleship relationship to meet every week is because we want people to understand the spirit of the law. The goal is to have meetings be consistent and intentional, but sensible in understanding that everyone's hectic schedules will not allow the rigidity to work.

Why is the one-on-one component important to our vision of discipleship? First, you are able to connect personally and build a relationship with those you are training. The nature of discipleship is intimate. It breeds vulnerability. You are opening up your life to another person and are allowing yourself to be held accountable.

These kinds of demands are extremely hard to maintain without trust, love, authenticity, and respect. It's hard to develop intimacy with another person without spending alone time with them.

Second, you do not have to overload your small group time because everyone knows that there is another consistent time devoted to growing personal relationship and practical ministry skills.

Here's a breakdown of what a busy week might look like with discipleship and small group obligations:

Meeting with Disciple #1 = 1.5 hrs
Meeting with Disciple #2 = 1.5 hrs
Meeting with Your Discipler = 1.5 hrs
Small Group = 2 hrs
Misc. Preparation = 2 hrs
Total Weekly Time (Max) = 8.5 hrs

The natural question is: can we really expect people to commit this much of their time to ministry in addition to their job and family obligations? The answer is yes. Traditionally, ministry has been viewed as being part of a small group and participating in various church programs throughout the week. When discipleship is implemented, people might think it is just another weekly program that's being thrown into the mix, another activity that they have to commit to. That's not the way it should be. By building conviction, discipleship doesn't have to be just another program on the periphery of the ministry but the life and blood of the ministry. We're not trying to add one more activity to people's hectic schedules; we're proposing that you discard programs that already unnecessarily exist and that you reassess your personal life and the ministry of your church or organization. True discipleship can't just be added to an existing process; it should be the nucleus of a ministry. The ministry has to restructure itself to accommodate the commitment that discipleship demands.

By no means am I suggesting that you cut out all programs and activities of your local church and solely have a discipleship ministry. I am merely suggesting that you assess what is accomplished through discipleship and what activities to discard if they are unable to offer the value that you assumed they would.

We must not work harder, but smarter, to ensure that people will grow in the Lord and flourish in ministry without ending up burned out or resenting the local church.

Small Group

The second component of discipleship is the commitment to a small group, or MACC Group as we call it at Mack Ave.[1]

MACC Groups are local, urban, diverse, missional communities of people that gather weekly to share life and truth, love God and one another, and engage the social and spiritual needs of our community. They are grounded in four principles that are shaped by four practices.

The Four Principles:
We are all broken.
> We are all more broken than we want to admit, and God is more holy than we can comprehend.

We all need Jesus.
> In Jesus, we are more forgiven and accepted than we can imagine, and God is more delighted in us than we understand.

We all need one another.
> We need each other to share our struggles and joys in following Jesus.

The world needs the Gospel.
> The Gospel offers the hope of justice, the clarity of truth, the comfort of grace, and the joy of Jesus to a broken world.

The Four Practices

SHARE	→	Truth and life
PRAY	→	For one another and the city
ENGAGE	→	People and culture
LOVE	→	One another

How Does It Work?
MACC Groups begin with a two-hour weekly commitment. We gather with no more than four families. During this time we share a meal, communion, and our hearts. Facilitated by a leader, our time together includes prayer and discussing the weekly message and/or book of the Bible.

The dinner responsibility is rotated weekly. The expectation is that these groups would be loving, simple, real, biblical, and missional. Once every four weeks, MACC Groups serve their local communities through MACC Outreach.

The Focus of Our Discussion:
God – What does the text say about God and His character?
Community – What does the text say about me and His people?
Missional – What does this text reveal about our context as missionaries?

Multiplying
The expectation is that each family is willing to lead a MACC Group when appropriate. This means either leaving their current group to start another or continuing with that group while starting another. This decision is jointly based on the desire of their group and discernment of the families.

STEP 7: ASSESS EACH DISCIPLE

Whether you are just beginning the process of discipleship or adding to an existing procedure, we have to realize that one specific discipleship strategy does not fit every ministry or person. For example, the path of a mature believer who is beginning to be discipled will look different than that of a new believer. Allowing each discipler to have the freedom to assess the needs of the disciple and arrange a discipleship plan based on the level of maturity of each person is crucial to having an effective discipleship lifestyle.

Although the discipleship process will look different depending on the maturity of the believer, what remains constant is that we know where we want all believers to eventually be: able to walk by faith, communicate their faith, and multiply their faith. We must assess what is needed to get them there.

Discerning Maturity

The best approach in identifying the spiritual maturity of a person is for them to be assessed by their discipler. This doesn't mean that the discipler quizzes them on theology or probes them with weird tests. The assessment can be done only when a platform is built. The discipler builds a relationship with the disciple and allows time for trust and understanding to organically take root. This needn't be a hasty process, but it must be on the discipler's agenda.

Provided below is a description of the three general levels of discipleship maturity that you will find in a person:

Discovery: The discovery stage is where individuals, after being assessed by their discipler, have little or no knowledge of what it means to walk by faith, communicate their faith, or multiply their faith. The discipler's focus is to spend time equipping the disciple in the fundamental truths of the faith and increasingly growing them in each area (word, relationship, and ministry) until maturity is developed. At this stage, the majority of time will be spent learning how to walk by faith. The next stage in development will be learning how to communicate and ultimately multiply their faith.

Training: The training stage is where basic maturity is confirmed by the discipler. At this stage, the disciple should possess an understanding of the Bible and consistently show that they desire and trust the Lord.

Although this person is walking with the Lord, it is common to lack practical training in Bible study skills, evangelism, and training on how to multiply their lives in Christ. By spending time in prayer and building a relationship with the disciple, the discipler should focus on assessing the disciple's strengths and areas of weakness.

As you learn how to best care for your disciple, continue to provide encouragement in their strengths while providing the opportunity for growth in areas of weakness. Use what you learn to specifically cater your discipleship time to best grow them holistically in Christ.

At this stage, your discipleship time will include at some point all three levels of training and development (walking, communicating and multiplying their faith). Because the disciple is becoming more of a self-feeder, you will spend most of your time training them on how to communicate and multiply their faith.

Spiritual Direction: At this stage, the person is a mature believer in Christ. They are walking by faith and have the capacity to begin to disciple someone else. They may still lack practical training on how to intentionally communicate and ultimately multiply their faith. Therefore, time should be focused on training them specifically how to evangelize and how to intentionally and holistically disciple someone.

At this stage, the goal of the discipler is to ensure that the mature believer still has accountability. We need to make certain that the disciples are in a place where they are flourishing in ministry by continually growing in their own personal walk with the Lord. The discipler needs to testify that the disciples are multiplying their lives by leading a discipleship group and teaching people how to walk by faith, communicate, and multiply their faith through the process of word, relationship, and ministry.

STEP 8: MAKE IT HAPPEN

Take a step of faith and live out the conviction that the Holy Spirit has put on your heart to "make disciples."

GO AND MAKE DISCIPLES

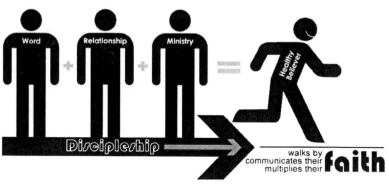

DISCIPLESHIP: TAKING GOD AT HIS WORD

I became convicted about the mandate of discipleship while I was in college. Though, I have to admit, it was more of a personal conviction. I was not yet convinced that Jesus' command was for all believers.

While in seminary, I befriended a professor who had been teaching on the subject of discipleship longer than I had been alive. What puzzled me, though, was his practical demonstration of discipleship. He required his students to disciple others but left "discipling" up to their interpretation. As long as we were meeting with another Christian on a regular basis, the professor assented that we were practicing discipleship. This challenged my understanding of discipleship. I was under the impression that discipling someone meant sharing our faith together, training in the Word, and teaching someone how to make disciples of his own. Was the professor being lax or was my view of discipleship too rigid and intense?

When I started spending more time at the Center for Disciple Building on campus, I noticed that there was great spiritual formation taking place but no training on how to minister or multiply one's faith. I remember thinking to myself, "Is this place missing a key component of discipleship, or am I the one that is off base?" Maybe I needed to lighten up.

In an attempt to clear things up, I underwent intense research on the biblical basis for discipleship. Upon turning in my paper, the professor told me that my exegesis was correct. This only made things stranger. If my exegesis was right, then the previous people I had encountered were off base. But I didn't want to be misunderstood as the guy who tells individuals and churches that they're doing it all wrong. I didn't want to come off as judgmental. That wasn't my heart.

When the team and I came to Detroit in 2007 and shared our vision of planting a discipleship-based ministry, other pastors in the community laughed at us. They said we'd never get enough members to keep our church afloat, that we'd scare too many people off. One pastor told me that the focus of our ministry should be on getting people into church on Sundays and wooing them with my personality and teaching. Despite the flack we were taking, the team remained convicted that we needed to focus on discipling and equipping others.

For the first couple of years, things were difficult. It took time and patience to disciple the first few individuals that we were beginning to journey with. We started with just four, and after a year it was eighteen, then thirty-eight after the second year. Today, we have well over fifty individuals in discipleship relationships. People want to be challenged and grow in Jesus. Now, other churches in the community are taking notice.

For the last four years, God has provided me with time to wrestle with the question: Is discipleship meant for the entire covenant community or is this just my preference? By God's grace, my conviction was reinforced.

Because of this, I couldn't shake the thought that the majority of churches in America are not making disciples, even though they think they are. I've spent many years trying to justify ministries that weren't making disciples and churches that didn't provide an environment where people learned how to make disciples.

Before we get defensive and show all the works we do and programs we have, can we humbly and soberly permit the possibility that we are not making disciples?

To be clear, I'm not saying that I am right and everybody else is wrong. I know there are churches that make disciples. I know a few personally.

I'm not trying to cast aspersions on your local church body or you as a leader. But my fear is that, after reading this book, some will try to justify and rationalize their ministry and defend it as discipleship. With grace, let me ask you to do something. Pull off the rose colored glasses. Take a serious look at yourself and your ministry.

You might be able to name five, ten, fifteen or twenty spiritual studs in your church body. But is the culture of your ministry one that makes disciples? Are you intentionally training people to be ministers of the Gospel and multipliers of their faith? Are you seeing people come to Christ and teaching them in everything He said? Is the weakest link of your church body being challenged to be all they can be in Christ?

If you or your ministry agrees that discipleship is biblical, but you want to do it in a less 'intense' way than I've modeled, then I absolutely still celebrate that. Do discipleship with your own flavor, according to the rhythm of your ministry. All I ask is that you adhere to what Christ is asking of you. As long as you are building intimate relationships, training people in the Word, and equipping them to communicate and multiply their faith, then by all means, get creative. There isn't one exact correct methodology, just a specific kind of intentionality.

Christ is calling us from the sidelines to the front line. We need to grab hold of the reality that He has sent us to fulfill His last words and make disciples of all nations. It's not an option. It's doctrine.

It is my prayer that churches, Christian organizations, and individuals start making disciples; that we live up to our name as the salt of the earth, light of the world, and fishers of men; that when we arrive at the understanding that we are sent by Christ, we actually go.

And make disciples.

MAKE A MOVE

Please consider holding your local leaders accountable to be making disciples in our communities.

Hopefully these questions will help you as you either begin this journey of discipleship or continue in the journey of discipleship.

Questions to encourage movement

Consider your environment:
1. Think about the church you attend. Do they take serious the things you have read?

2. Do they take the command of making disciples serious?
2a. If not, are they teachable to do so?

3. What are ways you can prayerfully and respectfully help your church engage in making disciples?

4. If you're not in an environment that is serious about equipping healthy, multiplying believers (or desiring to grow in this), consider finding a new church.

Consider your training:
1. Is there a list of men or women in your life that you would like to disciple you? Please write their names down.

2. Will you pray that the Lord would prepare his or her heart and within five days, approach the person and inquire about entering into a discipleship relationship? Start by reading this book and engage the discipleship process together. Seek to establish a balanced diet of word, relationship, and ministry in your relationship.

Consider your influence:
1. Is there someone in your life that you would like to disciple? Please write their names down.

2. Before approaching them allow scripture and the use of this book as a helpful tool to build theological conviction about what Jesus wants you to do with that person if you were to disciple them.

3. Set a date when you would like to approach that person about being discipled. Tell a friend and have them hold you accountable to that time frame.

Word, Relationship, and Ministry

1. Is one of these areas as discussed in the book lacking in your life?
If so, which one?

2. What steps will you take to seek being a healthy disciple?

Walking By Faith, Communicating your Faith and Multiplying your Faith

1. Are any of these areas a struggle for you as you walk with Jesus?
Which ones?

2. Who are the people you think that model what God wants in those respective areas?

3. Is there someone on your list that you can approach to help you gain health in that or those areas?

4. What is hindering you from beginning a discipleship chain in your community or church?

Thank You!

We hope God's people would begin to take the command "Make Disciples" personal. Please consider two people you know that would benefit from this book and provide them with a copy in order to encourage others in fulfilling their call to "Make Disciples."

Thanks and may Jesus be our treasure!

NOTES

CHAPTER 1: WE ARE MAKING DISCIPLES

1. This book is written on the shoulders of people who discussed this topic before I was born. This book is not about notoriety or originality but faithfulness to the clear things of God.

CHAPTER 2: THE BIBLICAL RATIONAL FOR DISCIPLESHIP

1. *Theological dictionary of the New Testament, Volume 1* By Gerhard Kittel, Gerhard Friedrich, Geoffrey William Bromiley pg 560.

2. *The New Bible Dictionary*, (Wheaton, Illinois: Tyndale House Publishers, Inc.) 1962.

3. Thanks to Dr. Tennent who taught us holistically about The Great Commissions.

4. Mark 16 does not appear in the two major manuscripts (MSS) of the New Testament: the Codex *Sinaiticus* and Codex *Vaticanus*. Therefore it is questionable if it should be seen as original to the Gospel.

5. Daniel B. Wallace, *Greek Grammar Beyond The Basics: An Exegetical Syntax of the New Testament*. (Grand Rapids: Zondervan Publishing House, 1996), 645.

6. Wallace, 529.

7. I wrote this clearly from a believer's baptism perspective. I want to encourage you to research other traditions of thought that are not represented i.e. paedobaptist.

8. Dr. Robert E. Coleman, *The Master Plan Of Evangelism* (New Jersey: Fleming H Revell Company, 1964).

CHAPTER 3: WHY WE DISCIPLE

1. Thanks to Roger for teaching me Word, Relationship, and Ministry.

CHAPTER 4: THE WORD IN DISCIPLESHIP

1. George Barna, http://www.barna.org.

CHAPTER 5: MINISTRY IN DISCIPLESHIP

1. The Alpha Course, 2009-20011, http://alphausa.org.

2. John Piper, *Let the Nations Be Glad! The Supremacy of God in Missions*, 2nd Ed. (Grand Rapids: Baker, 1993/2003), 17.

3. Bill Bright's famous definition of evangelism.

CHAPTER 9: DISCIPLESHIP STEP BY STEP

1. This was given to Mack Avenue from my dear friend Jonathan Dodson and the Gospel centered body of Austin City Life.